Uncommon

A Black Man's Journey

Revised Version

By Mel King

Plus, a Bonus Feature

"Go-Kart & the Night"

About the Author

Mel is a Baby Boomer, Black, and grew up in South Central Los Angeles in the 60's and 70's. He has an MBA from Loyola Marymount University and currently reside in Pennsylvania. He had many challenges throughout his life encountering discrimination, mostly in the subtle, non-overt way. He has made millions for the corporate bottom-line, but received little recognition. On several occasions, he became the lead negotiator for companies in the aerospace industry. It was not in his job description; however, it was noted, in each instance, that the companies experienced its best performance in contract acquisitions and profit. Knowing that he frequently outperformed his peers, and received little recognition, he indicates that it is painful to see, in today's society, people being promoted or appointed to a position, not based on capability, but on their beliefs, skin color, or association.

High School

Graduation, ah yes graduation. I have just completed three great years at Manual Arts High in South Central Los Angeles. The school went from the tenth to the twelfth grade. As a tenth grader the school was frightening, intimidating, and imposing, now I look back at the school, and those years, lovingly and with fond affection. I have little to say or remember about my sophomore year, other than I lettered in swimming. Well, I can tell you a brief story about swimming.

Swimming

Manual Arts, at the time, was transitioning from an all-white school to where it was about 30% white and 70% black. During this time, one of the athletic coaches wanted to start a new swim team and was looking for swimmers. He wanted a young team so that he could spend a couple years training prior to graduation. The new and hopeful swimming coach asked the honored selectees if any of us knew how to swim. Nary a hand went up. As I mentioned, the school was in transition. Most of the younger students, including myself, were black. Ever hear of a black person that knew how to swim, that lived in the city? Even though we lived in beautiful, L.A. (Los Angeles), sunshine and all, I didn't know one black person that had a pool. White either for that matter (one of my best friends was white). Well, when the coach couldn't find any true swimmers, he asked "how many of you have 'played' in the water?" At that my hand went up.

Every summer we used to go to the L.A. swimming stadium that was built for the 1932 Olympics. It was open to the public during the summer and it cost $0.25 to get in. There were two pools actually. One, that we called the wading pool, went from six inches to four feet. Anyone could "play" in this pool. However, many of us would stand at the surrounding fence of the Olympic sized pool and say, "one day." You see, you had to pass a test to get into the "big pool." The big pool had one end of it roped off.

To pass the test to enter, a swimmer had to swim all the way across and back, lingering no more than three seconds when they touch the other side. The distance was, maybe 25 yards, but seemed like a mile. With a long pole, fashioned with a hoop, life guards were constantly pulling people out of the water, and yet, people kept trying. Me and all my buddies made a vow that someday we would pass the test.

Now here I am, in front of a swimming coach, with him saying that I am on the swimming team. Now you don't know how intimidating this is until you realize two things: 1) It was only two summers ago that I "passed the test"; and 2) we were going to have to swim the pool several times… the Lo-o-o-ng way. Under the coach's coaching, I progressed rapidly and was swimming freestyle, backstroke and breaststroke multiple times down the length of the pool.

The pool was outdoors, with no heater, and, on one day, it was a cold morning in L.A. as we were getting ready to swim. As I looked at the pool, I swear I could see ice cubes forming on the water. I went over to the pool and stuck my big toe in the water. Instant frostbite. I looked at the coach, looked at the water, looked at the coach again. At that moment, to me, I made a life-saving decision. I looked at the coach and said, "Coach, I'm not getting in the water today." If the cold water had not frozen the team, my comment did. I'm sure the coach didn't believe what he heard either, as he asked me to repeat what I said.

I said, "Coach, I'm not getting in the water today, it's too cold."

There was still no movement from the team. The only sound that could be heard was the gentle lapping of the water against the side of the pool. The coach continued to stare at me, then he went over to the pool, bent down, stuck his hand in the water.

"Mel you're right, the water is cold." The coach said. Then the coach looked at everyone else. "Since you guys didn't complain, everybody else, into the pool."

I made a lot of friends that day. Yeah, right! A short time later, the coach came over to me as I was sitting beside the surrounding fence, about 15 feet from the pool.

"Well Mel, you gotta do something, so why don't you sit over here by the side of the pool and help me keep track of the laps the guys are swimming. Here's a pen and clip board."

I got up, moved over to the side of the pool. I was fat, dumb, and happy. Sitting beside the pool, I was keeping meticulous count of each lap by each swimmer. Suddenly, I saw a flicker of a shadow pass by me. In panic I started to get up. Too late. I'm in the air. In slow motion, I looked around and saw, magically, everyone was at the end of the pool, no one was swimming, and all eyes were on me. As I began to descend from the apex of my parabolic arc, I could see smiles slowly beginning to form on all the faces that were in that cold, cold water. I dreaded the thought that I would soon join them, not in the smile, but in that cold, cold water. Ker-splash, I hit the water. My head, my back, my butt, my … well I don't think I want to be too descriptive. Anyhow, I felt that water enveloped my body inch by incredibly cold inch. When I surfaced, all I heard was laughter. I think the coach was laughing the loudest. I crawled out like a wet puppy.

The coach looked at me and said, "Since you're all wet you may as well swim a few laps to warm up." To this day, I don't like cold water.

Southern League, our sports division, had four out of the six schools whose students were predominantly black. Fremont, Jefferson, Manual Arts, and Dorsey, for the most part, were "Black" schools, with Fremont and Jefferson being about 100%. The other two schools, Washington and LA High were mixed with about 30% black students. This racial mix is important. Remember what I said about Black guys and swimming. Well, our event with Jefferson was very memorable. I'll describe what happened in one event. It was the 400-meter distance swim. There were six competitors, three from our school and three from Jefferson. The first 200 meters were uneventful except that our three team members had an exceptional lead over the other team. What happened the last 200 meters challenged our sportsman's creed. One of Jefferson's swimmers, who swam next to the edge of the pool began to exhibit a new stroke. He would stroke with one arm, grab the side of the pool with the other, stroke, grab, stroke, grab. We all wanted to go into hysteria, but then there was coach. We could tell he was about to lose it as well and we didn't want to display poor sportsmanship.

In our practices thereafter, the coach would jokingly say to anyone that was slacking off; "Come on, come on, let's stop doing the Jefferson stroke."

Sports/ Extra Curricular Activities

In my 11th year of school, I was a sports writer for the school, on the swimming team, "B" football team, and was a member of the Cooperative Cabinet. My tenure as a Co-op Cabinet member and ultimately, it's elected President came at the encouragement of Mr. Hayes, during the latter part of my 10th grade semester. Mr. Hayes was my Industrial Arts teacher and provided oversight to the Cooperative Government Cabinet that was ran by students. During the course of my Industrial Arts class, Mr. Hayes was often impressed by my drawing talents. He frequently displayed my 3-D renderings of our 2-D mechanical drawing projects. With his encouragement, I signed up to be a non-elected member of Cooperative Government. Because of Mr. Hayes, my junior year was my coming out year in high school. My senior semester, I believe was over the top.

I did very well in sports in my senior year.

First there was swimming. I lettered in swimming and four of us qualified to compete in state competition. Competing at State was a long way from that cold morning when I wanted to boycott the training and got thrown in the pool. Moreover, it said something about our coach and what he was able to do with the pool of kids in which he had to draw from. We didn't do well at State, but we had an opportunity never given to the school before; and, we didn't come in last.

Secondly, I also lettered in "B" football playing center, and made, "All-Southern League" first team honors for the league. This level had a weight limit of 160 lbs. and had quite a following. The stands were fuller than junior varsity football but not as full as varsity. Still, there were sufficient numbers of people to make a lot of noise in the stands when we played. Unfortunately, no one from the family ever attended any of the swim meets or football games to add to the cacophony. I had a lot of friends come though, of which I was very appreciative.

In my Senior Semester, I continued to be a Sports Writer, had joined the Knights, was on Boys Court, President of Co-op Cabinet (an elected position), a member of Student Body Cabinet and made the Honor Roll. Oh, and worked nights and Saturdays. I think back on all that I did and were involved in, and honestly, I'm amazed and humbly impressed. I thank God for Mr. Hayes. He saw something in me that no other person took time to notice, or if they did, did not invest the time to nurture what was locked up inside. His guidance was extremely important. For example, one day I was doing my rounds, checking in with all the hall monitors. Hall monitors were student volunteers that sat at the entrance to all school doors monitoring the incoming and outgoing of students during the time class was in session. They had the authority to issue citations or detention slips if a student did not have approval to be out of class. As I was making my rounds, I checked on this one hall monitor.

"How is your day going?" I said.

"It has been very quiet, no problems." She said.

"That is great, let me know if you ever need something."
With that I turned around, saw Mr. Hayes, and went over to speak to him. After our discussion, I proceeded to go out the nearest door. The hall monitor had a fit.

"Don't go out that door!" She said.

"Why not? Is something wrong with it?"

"No, but I only have this one door for coming and going. That way I can monitor the students better."

"But I am the President." I spoke.
At that point, Mr. Hayes, who had been witnessing this interchange, called me over to speak with him.

"Mel, why didn't you want to comply with her request to use the one door?"

"Because I am the President, and she reports to me."

"That is true Mel, you are the President and she does report to you. And, it is because you are the President that you should honor those that work for you."
Ouch, that hurt. He went on to talk about the difference between a leader and a great leader.

"As a leader, it's crucial to honor and respect those who work for you. True leadership isn't about asserting authority, but about inspiring and supporting others. Do you want to be a great leader?"

"Yes, I do."

"Then go over and apologize for your action."

I thought for a second, "Do I really want to be a great leader?"
Mr. Hayes was my faculty advisor in my position, as President of Cooperative Government, and I highly valued his comments and advice. With tongue in cheek, I went back to the hall monitor and

apologized for being rude and unsupportive. Her expression was worth the apology. From that point on I could do no wrong in her sight.

A couple of days later as I was leaving the building in which she had hall monitoring duty, she called out, "Mel you can use the other door if you want."

"No thanks. Wouldn't want to set a precedent. And besides, wouldn't want to ruin your reputation, people may begin to think you're a pushover." We both laughed, and I thanked her for the job she was doing.

Two Friends

Mi dos amigos, Greg, Red and myself quietly became three of the most influential but little-known seniors on the campus. Greg was the Boy's Court judge; Red was responsible for detention or the "jailor" and my office was akin to the DA. I caught 'em, Greg tried 'em, and Red jailed 'em. How impacting this was on students became apparent when a male student was in one of the buildings without a "hall-pass." I saw him, asked him to stop, but he began to run. It just so happened that Greg and Red were coming in the door as he was approaching from the opposite side. They saw him running and me chasing. They were quick on the uptake. Greg was 6'2" and about 210. Red was about 5'10, but stocky. Greg just blocked the door. Red stood to one side to keep him from trying another door. The offending student looked at Greg just once and decided that he would stand a better fate if he faced me and got a citation. I wrote him the citation to appear in Boys Court for his "hearing." As I was writing, he was bragging the whole time.

"You guys just wait. I know people, even teachers in high places. They will take care of you and that citation. I'm going to get off, so you are just wasting your time in writing a ticket." He said.

The day he shows up in court, he sees Greg as the presiding Judge and Red as the Bailiff. The guy wasn't dumb. He looked at Greg, looked at Red, then he looked at me.

Finally, he said, "OK, how much time."

Since he didn't continue his braggadocio attitude, I pleaded his case to get a reduced sentence and it was granted. From that day forward we became friends. And, from that day forward, he did know people in high places. Well, at least at school.

Seagulls

Los Angeles is the "City of Angels," but it is also the city of "Seagulls." Seagulls are as numerous in L.A. as pigeons are in most other cities; excepting seagull have a nasty habit of making bomb runs.   Pigeons rarely poop on the fly, but seagulls are different. Since seagulls spend a lot of time over water, and no place to land, they often poop while flying. In fact, I don't think they know how to poop sitting still. Well, I think you know where this is going. Yep, one day one of my fellow students was just standing around outside with a few friends during lunch. No one was permitted to be in the buildings during lunch since some classes were still in session. So, everyone had their little spot where they gathered, ate, and talked with friends. Also, hall passes were needed to be in the building during lunch time.

As Co-op Government President (CGP), I had just walked outside after doing my rounds checking on the hall and building monitors. When I looked up into the sky, I saw a flock of seagulls flying, and the manner in which they were flying reminded me so much of a dive bomber formation of WWII era. I was so intrigued that I stood there and just watched them fly. For some unknown reason I began to watch this one seagull in particular, don't know why, maybe my subconscious knew that he was flying differently than the rest. Anyhow, with a grace that is hard to describe, this one seagull caught a little more wind than the others. Head up, wings in an elevated angle, tail feathers flaring, just a little, he pulled out of formation and began his own circling. Now I really got curious. He raised one wing and dipped the other in a beautiful pirouette that changed his direction without any apparent loss in speed or altitude. Amazing. Then this seagull obviously set a purposeful track, as if he had dead-reckoning radar. I could see the seagull stick up one feather checking wind direction and speed, followed by a little course correction.   At the nadir of his slow, shallow curve.... The targeted student immediately jumped as his hand began the slow dreaded rise to his head, hoping that what happened didn't happen. His worst fears were realized as he saw the seagull wag his wings back and forth and do a barrel roll, signifying a successful, on target drop.   The student was in a dilemma. Lunch had just started; he didn't have a hall pass and now he has seagull poop on his head.

With a straight face I hurried up to the guy, and stopped his hand just before confirmation, and said; "Your worst fear just happened. But I can get you into the building to clean up."

With a sigh and obvious relief, he let me escort him to the hall and doorway monitor. I OK'd him to go to the restroom.   To save him from embarrassment, I didn't say why he should be permitted to go to the restroom. Oddly enough no one else seemed to have noticed what happened; not even the group of people with whom he was standing. All the while I was thinking, except for a few more steps, there goes I.

Junior Cops

Part of my responsibility, as Co-op Government President, was the policing of students that were off campus when they shouldn't be. In order to execute this policing, I would gather up some of the biggest guys on my staff and would deputize some of the biggest football players in the school. This was heady stuff. Just think, I had the authority to take six to eight guys into any building on campus, pass door and hallway monitors, and out into the streets…Freedom! The guys that went with me would revel in this seemingly impossible opportunity…on the streets, weekday, during school hours, no punishment. Wow! Once outside the school doors, first time football players wouldn't leave it to chance, but would immediately begin petitioning to be a part of the next team that ventures out.   With this deputized bunch of guys, we would patrol all the hamburger and hotdog stands for about ½ mile in either direction on Vermont and Santa Barbara (now King Blvd). Anytime we met someone that should be in school, we would give them a citation, which would result in their attending either Boy's or Girl's Court and ultimately some form of detention. Since we performed these patrols at lunchtime, and we were missing our own, we worked out a plan (some would call it a scheme) to get a free lunch. If we observed a group ordering a meal, we would wait outside. When the order was placed and paid for then we would approach the group, presented our ID cards which indicated who we were. We took their name and gave each a citation and told them that they had to report back to the school immediately.

"But we just placed an order and paid for it," they protested.

"If you don't leave now, you get a second citation, which may double the detention time, your choice," was often our reply. The owners of these establishments began to become acquainted with our antics and had no problem of turning the hamburgers over to us as "evidence." It is truly amazing how power can insinuate itself and cause someone to believe that they are above the law. I had to fight this sneaky snake constantly.

On one patrol, we spotted a student, probably one of the most well known in the school, outside of the school property.

He spotted us at a distance and yelled, "Scatter, here comes the Junior Cop."

I had never thought about us being junior cops, but it certainly depends on who is doing the looking. As with most hunters, it is either the weakest or the trophy that is sought. We went after the trophy, and bagged him we did. Being one of the most well-known students has its advantages, but also, its disadvantages, you can't fade into the background noise. We no sooner walked back on campus after our patrol that it was obvious the pebble had dropped into the pond. The gossip waves were spiraling outward in an ever increasing, larger circle. We heard that we had ganged up on the guy and beat him into submission; also, he held off the group of us until a couple of other junior cops entered the fray and turned the tide. Not that we were trying to keep our identity a secret, however this capture threatened to give us more exposure than we ever wanted. Did we think about the exposure when we went after the trophy? Nah. We were teenagers. Whoever heard of teenagers connecting the dots?

Dance

One day in a Student Body Cabinet meeting, the subject of fund raising came up to help the school buy a marquee. Since Greg and I both were on the cabinet and sat beside one another, we spoke briefly and offered one recommendation. Sell old 45's (record disc) for $0.25 apiece. New, they cost about $0.49 - $0.79 apiece on average. Just to give some idea what $0.25 was at the time: Gas was $0.25/gal; bread was $0.17; Cigarettes were $0.25; and a pack of gum was $0.05. The initial reaction of the Cabinet was that of derision.

"Who would want to buy old, outdated records?" "Who would pay that much for something so old?" On and on went the comments.

Greg and I didn't respond, other than to say, "It was just an idea." Well, the next cabinet meeting, Greg and I brought in a box of the old records. "Maybe," "Duke of Earl," and "Why do fools fall in love?" where just a few of the titles we read to the Cabinet members. Immediately they began to ask if they could purchase the records right then and there.

We reminded them that "No one would want to buy old, out of date records." However, we limited each Cabinet member to purchase one each of their choice. The rest we made available to sell at lunch time to the entire student body. The collection didn't last long. There were probably 300 records in the entire collection.

The second part of our suggestion was to take the money from the record sell, buy more recent hits and start a "Noon Dance." We would charge $0.10 per student as an entry fee. The first day of the dance made Greg and I wonder if this was such a good idea. As good entrepreneurs do, we made an adjustment. We needed momentum and we needed it fast. We made an announcement that the first 50 girls and 25 guys would be free for the next three days. We knew if the girls were there, the guys would come. And come they did. Now that we had people attending, we had to get them to dance. But, that wasn't really too much of a problem. You see, Greg, Red and I had long worked out a routine to get parties started. We would arrive at a party, see all the girls on one side of the room, all the guys on the other. We would "scope out" the ladies, find the ones that appeared friendly, and have them prepped. Meanwhile, one of us would commandeer the record player and play the most popular slow record available. If nothing else the three of us would be dancing with the girls we selected. However, I don't ever recall where we failed to get a party going using this process.

It got to the point where we were assured invites, just because people knew we would kick-start a party if it wasn't going by the time we got there. Well, the first couple of noon dances were no different. The boys had lined up on the east wall of the gym, the girls on the west. We had to go into our party starting mode. Same result. It didn't take long before east met west. Within the second month, we had over 100 people in the gymnasium and it wasn't too long thereafter that we were consistently having 200+ people in attendance. The fund raising was going very well. The school was divided into two lunch breaks, so we were able to take advantage of both time periods for the dances.

On one Catholic holiday, one of the girls that belonged to the "group" that Greg, Red and I hung out with, away from school, had heard about the Noon Dance and wanted to come. Power is a relative thing. For a school, I had power. But again, power is a heady thing. Fortunately, I tried not to let it get to my head, although there were times when I would let a little slip through. Our friend, Deborah came up to the school at the appointed time. Mind you, there were no cell phones then to coordinate timing. So, she had to be there on time or I would miss her. Deborah is at the door, I come, I speak to the door monitor, the door opens, in walks Deborah. As I said, power is a heady thing. When you think of it, no other student in the school could have done what I just did. Wow! I walk Deborah through the building and courtyard to the gym. I arrived just in time to open the doors and greet people as they come in. Of course, Greg, Red, and I were in charge of the event and made quite an impression on Deborah. We were very certain that she would tell her friends at the Catholic school, oh yea!

A need for Financial Independence

Sometime near the end of my sophomore year of high school my dad disappeared. The family had no idea where he may have gone. With his disappearance, the family finances went into a tailspin. I never had an abundance of money, and now with dad gone, my ability to participate in school or weekend activities was at zero. There was only one thing to do. Find a job. It took me a couple of months but I did find something.   The job was a part-time job at a produce company. I straightened and cleaned the produce bins, swept the floors, and took out the trash. I started at $0.50/ hr. This was at a time when gas was $0.25/ gal, and bread was $0.17 a loaf. A person could go to the movies, have popcorn and a drink for a dollar. In my senior year I began making deliveries on the weekend. There were a many of times when I made deliveries that the warehouse people on the receiving end would come out with a perplexed look on their face. I would ring a bell, someone would come out, and what they saw was an oversized bobtail truck (tandem wheels in the back), and a 155-pound kid that looked like he was 14.

I think their first thoughts when they saw me was, "What is this kid doing on our docks, better get him off and on his way." However, they would ask me, "Where is the driver?"

With a smile, I would say, "I am."

"No Way!" would be their immediate response.

"Yep, got the Bill of Lading (BOL) right here." The dock man would be shaking his head the whole time he was unloading and even more so when he would sign the BOL.

I would take my copy and with a cheerful, "See ya next time," and be on my way.

I worked at this company my entire junior and senior year.

I was very thankful for the job as it permitted me to go to both my junior and senior prom, buy a class ring, class sweater, and go to occasional parties on the weekend. I even contributed some monies to needs of the household.

Basic Training

It was a quick trip to LAX, the Los Angeles airport one summer day. Not that it was quick regarding time, but in that my mind was all over the place as I couldn't focus on any one thing, except one, I'm going into the Air Force. My sister, Victoria, was driving. Although she is a couple of years older, I usually did the driving whenever we went anyplace. I was seventeen, but had already been driving for a couple of years. My mom didn't drive, so I had a special license to drive her around. This went over real great with my friends. All we needed was access to a car, so we constantly scrounged around to see who could get a vehicle. There weren't too many weekends where we didn't have any "wheels.' But see how my mind is bouncing around.

We arrive at the airport and I thought, "how did I end up here at this place, at this time?"

It started with Red, yep, my buddy Red. In the 11th grade we talked about joining the Air Force under their "Buddy" program. When we became seniors in high school, we went to talk with an Air Force recruiter and he told us about this new commitment program. You can sign up for the service while a senior in high school, and, upon graduation you have up to three months before you would have to report for basic training. And yes, they would honor the Buddy Program as well. Red and I took whatever info that the recruiter gave us and we said we would be back in touch. A couple of days go by and I ask Red what he was going to do. He said he was going down tomorrow to sign up. I said, "in that case, I'll go down this afternoon since I have to work tomorrow night." "OK, I'll check with you tomorrow to find out how it went." Well, two days go by and no Red. When I talked with him on the third day, I told him I had signed up, and asked how his trip to the recruiter went.

"Oh, I forgot to go." He responded.

"Forgot to go?" I said.

Now I was really seeing red. There I go day-dreaming again. Anyhow, I got on a plane (my first commercial plane ride) heading to Amarillo, Texas. We first flew into San Antonio, and then from there, got on a bus to Amarillo.

There were a bunch of us on a Greyhound bus with very few civilians. I don't remember if I really thought in a military way to make a distinction of "civilian," however, it was apparent those that were going to basic training and those who were not. At the base, we signed in and the Drill Instructor (DI) wasted no time in letting us know that he was boss.

"My oh my, why did Uncle Sam waste his money on the likes of you? They ought to pay me double time just to stand in front of ya. It's amaaazing the stuff they can dig up these days."

We were still in civies, (civilian clothes) which is different from skivvies (underwear), and the DI had us in a loose formation (we were too green to make it tight), running to the admin building to complete sign-in, running to get our boots, running to get our shirts and pants, and running to get our hair cut.

"All right let's see if you guys know yer left from yer right, and know what a formation looks like. Gimme a straight line next to that building over yonder."

We turned around to see which building he was talking about. It was about 100 yards away. We began walking toward the building.

Did I say walk?

He didn't say run either, but none of us was going to correct him. We ran to the building and stood in a straight line.

"All right now listen up cuz I know this is going to be real complicated for you. Look to your left, if you are taller than the person to your left, move him to your right. Oh, mama mia, I must be in purgatory. Really, where did you guys come from? You, are you taller than the person on your left?"

"Yeh."

"Oh no I didn't. I know I didn't hear a 'Yeh.' Did any of you little chickens hear a 'Yeh' come out of the mouth of this little hatchling? "No, I didn't think so." "What I thought I heard was 'Yes, Sir!' Isn't that what you heard?"

"Yes, Sir" said all of us in some sort of unison

"What?" The DI asked again.

"YES, SIR!" We responded, louder

"What?

"**YES, SIR!**" We exclaimed at the top of our voices.

"That's what I thought I heard."

With his establishing his superiority, he then began instructing us to form a loose formation.

"You! Hatchling, the little guy what is now the front of the line. You are the shortest one here and have the honor of being number one. If you are number one, what do you think the guy next to you is?"

"Number two?"

"You all look like number two to me. It's not just number two, its number two, Sir. What do you think the guy next to him is?"

"Number three, Sir."

"My, My, it is amaaazing what intelligence you can squeeze out of a hatchling these days. Now that you heard that the first three are one, two, and three, do you think the rest of you can count? I'll give you a hint. You, number four, why don't you start."

"Four" the trainee said.

"Four, what?"

"Four, Sir"

Next. The DI said.

"Five, Sir. Six, Sir. Seven Sir. . . 100 Sir."

Remarkable that you ladies can count. Now I want you to count from one to ten and start over, repeating from one to ten. Can you ladies do that for me?"

"Yes Sir."

"Now I want all of you to turn to your right and look at the head in front of you. Oh no you didn't. Did you turn left? Of course, you did. You got something going with the fella behind you? Why are you looking at his face? Turn around dummy and face the other way. Now, I want all the "ones" to stay where they are, number two's, line up to the left of number one that is directly in front of you. Number three, you do the same. Guess what you number's four and five are supposed to do?

"We are to line up…" a trainee started to say.

"Who asked your opinion? When I want you to talk, I will ask you to talk. All I want from you is action, boy, action."

When we completed this last step, we were in a loose formation, 10 rows with 10 across. We didn't know at the time, but what we did established our permanent position within the "Flight."   We would maintain this place within the Flight until graduation.

We later realized, after being at the base for a while, that the DI didn't always take the shortest route on that first day. Anyhow, it didn't take long for the days to settle into a routine. Up before dark, short PT (physical Training), Breakfast, Classes on survival training, weapons, types of aircraft, history of the Air Force, etc., PT, Lunch, Formation training, classes, PT, Dinner, barracks cleaning then lights out.   We were flight 3762nd.

One day, while jogging to class in formation, our sister flight just a few yards behind us, we approached an obstacle. The obstacle was a rather large bolder. Usually, we would go around a boulder this size, however, our sister flight was getting a little uppity lately, so…. Word was past through the ranks, boulder ahead, boulder ahead, etc., rank by rank. The boulder parted us, but wiped out about six wide and the first three rows of our sister flight. We kept running, after all, we didn't want to be late for class. At this time, I guess I should tell you what a sister flight is. In basic training, you would stay in fairly large dormitories, either three or four floors, divided by a day-room on the first floor but walled off on the other floors. There would be 100 guys to a flight, with two guys to a room. Within the flight, we would have a flight leader, sergeant of arms, barracks watch, and several other positions. The most coveted was the Dorm Chief (DC) position, who also was designated as the Flight Leader. The Flight Leader was effectively in charge when the DI or any other Air Force personnel of rank was not around. We competed with our sister flight in everything, class scores, shooting, obstacle course times, number of letters from home, if it was measured, we competed. The looser would have to buy ice cream for the winners on our half day off on

Sundays. I believe the respective DIs got in on the act as well. There were times when we lost out on timing at the obstacle course by just a few seconds. Boy, did our DI get mad. I mean madder than usual. Not the, I'm yelling at you because it is my job, mad, but you just cost me my house, my car, … my wife, mad. We did a three-mile run in full gear as a result. We didn't lose again on the obstacle course. In fact, that was a turning point for our flight. We began to get better and better than our sister flight in all that we did. However, we only had just a few weeks remaining so we were not going to show them up for too long. I got an expert rating (99 out of 100) while at the shooting range, so I got treated pretty good by the DI for the week, especially since we eked out a win by just a couple of points.

The Night before Graduation

Then there was the night before graduation day. Strange, but I remember the night before more than I remember the day. It was the night before graduation and we were all full of ourselves. We made it, we're bad, we're bad, uh-huh, we're bad. Well, it was dusk so a lot of us were in the day room reading, writing letters, watching TV. Nothing much happening, until.... For some reason our respective Dorm Chiefs (DC) started arguing with one another. Everyone cleared out of the Dayroom except those two. They began to wrestle with one another. Our Dorm Chief was Black, 6'2" and about 200 lbs, their Dorm Chief had a similar build, Italian and was from Detroit, so there was no weight or height advantage. And since we were at the end of our training, we all were probably at the best physical conditioning we ever were. So, this was going to be interesting (Note: I was 6' 0" and 160lbs.). They began to wrestle on the floor, across the sofa, against the chairs and almost into the TV. But neither was prevailing. I can't say how long this went on but both flights comprising of one hundred guys crammed doorways and windows to watch. Strange, can you imagine 200 guys watching, yelling screaming, but no one tried to intervene. During the wrestling, our Dorm Chief had managed to get the other DC close to our side of the dorm. No one entered into the dayroom, it just became understood that this was between the DCs and no intervention was allowed. However, as our DC brought the other DC closer to our side, the sister DC looked up, saw all these hands reaching for him... PANIC. He got this superhuman strength picked up our DC and carried him halfway across the room before our DC was able to trip him up. Slowly, their DC was able to get our DC close to the doorway on the other side of the dayroom where our sister flight had gathered. PANIC. Our DC in turn received this Herculean strength, picked up the sister DC and carried him toward our side of the dayroom. He made it about three quarters of the way before he fell. Still holding on to an arm, our DC was slowly dragging the sister DC to our doorway. At that point things begin to happen in slow motion.

Those of us standing in the doorway began reaching out to get our sister DC as our DC brought him closer. Members of our sister flight couldn't stand seeing their DC being "captured" by the enemy, like a worm being carried into an anthill. Just as we grab the DC arms of our sister flight, members of our sister flight left the doorway, crawled through windows and crossed the demilitarized zone or DMZ for short. The battle began. War was declared that day. I can't say all that ensued thereafter. If you can imagine 200 emotionally pent-up, virile, prime conditioned young men going at each other for a couple of hours, then you can imagine the damage to self and physical surroundings. It was a disaster. And we are to graduate in 16 hours. Yea, right. After the emotions were spent and we became physically exhausted, we all walked back and gathered in the dayroom. Yep, all 200 of us. Except for heavy breathing, not a word was spoken. Miraculously, no one had broken bones. Bruises, a few darkening eyes, yes, but nothing broken. In our mind, each of us saw the numerous holes in the walls, the DI walking through the war zone and declaring us unfit for graduation. We thought, the stupidity of youth. Living in the now, no thought of consequences. As we thought of what we did our heads began to hang lower and lower still.

I entered Basic training at the age of 17 and had my 18th birthday during my first month of training. I was the youngest airman of both flights. Yet, there are times in my life when I will take charge of a situation, expect compliance to orders and have the confidence to carry it out. This was one of those times. And of course, my tenure in high school as an elected official didn't hurt.

When our heads reached its nadir or lowest point, a solution came to mind that was as bright as the noonday sun. I stood up, commanded attention and laid out my idea. You see, I remembered that a couple of days ago I was walking back from another area on the base where we could go to use the telephone. While walking through the area I saw another dorm being built or renovated. Obviously, I didn't think much of it at the time. Now, however, it was going to be our salvation, our restoration, our graduation.

"Guys, I have a plan. A couple of days ago I saw another dorm being built or renovated about a quarter of a mile from here. In that dorm they have sheet rock. plaster, and paint. We have tape that we wrap packages in to send home, we have sponges to clean the latrine and floors with, and we have razor blades for multiple uses. With what is in that dorm and the things we have here, we can repair our dorm. All we have to do is to make the repairs last 24 hours. After that, we'll be scattered to the winds."

The dorm remained quiet for another 4-5 seconds then a cacophony of sound erupted that would pierce your eardrums. I asked for quiet once again and thankfully, the two DCs took charge to bring the room to order. I indicated we needed to breakup into groups of various work details. We had a group that would go and get the sheetrock, plaster and paint that we needed. While they were raiding the other dorm, we had a group that was going around cutting out and squaring off all the holes in the dorm with our single edged razor blades (and there was a bunch of holes). By the time the first group returned with the sheetrock, we had some of the holes cut and ready. We sized the sheetrock to the hole, took razor blade in hand and begin to cut. We placed the sheetrock in the hole, took the packaging tape, wet it with a sponge and taped the sheetrock in the hole. After each hole was done, we cleaned up all the debris around the hole and prepped the wall for spackling and painting. We applied the spackle with our hands and used rulers to even and smooth it out. Since the spackle took the longest to dry, we did what we could to get that done in a hurry. We repeated this process over and over again. Talk about adversity bringing unity, there was no hostility, no competition between the flights, all of us were working, side by side. All of us knew, if there was one discovery, the whole effort would crumble like a house of cards – no graduation. Lastly, we also used the sponges as paint brushes. Initially you probably thought, "what a neat idea." It was except for the paint that would lodge under the fingernails and be a potential give-away during next day's inspections. However, we had no choice. I don't remember how late we stayed up that night, but it was way past midnight before we finished. We took all the excess material back to the dorm under construction, cleaned the floors, and did a final walk through. We just couldn't afford to leave a trace of evidence. The morning wake-up call came way too early. We couldn't tell if we were excited about graduation... or the fact that we man not graduate, only time and the DI would tell.

As we got dressed, hopefully our final time, and stood at parade rest outside the dorm room, we waited for the DI. There was no joking, no talking, in fact no whispering even. Each and every one of us were fighting our own monsters, trying to hold back thoughts of what could happen with the discovery. I was on the first floor, so we were expecting to be inspected first. But DI's like to be un-predictable. The inspections began on the third floor and the DI of our sister flight inspected us while our DI inspected them. It's amazing how rapidly this fact became known to us, even without cell phones of today. I felt like I stayed at parade rest for three days. We were hearing all kinds of thumps, bumps and yelling coming from the upper floors and it didn't sound very good. In our minds, the monsters were let loose and were getting bigger and bigger and harder to control. Finally, the time arrived, the DI was on our floor. By now it was like, take me out and shoot me, get this over with. There I stood, the DI and I. Face to face. I wanted so much to break the tension, like wink at him or even a little smile, but oh boy would that be dumb. He continued to glare at me. Nothing said. Nothing moved.

Then he did a strange thing. He stepped back, looked at the rest of the squad down the hall and said, "Alright, all you @#$#@, go line up for graduation." No one moved. The DI then said, "Alright, if you like it here that much..."

He never got to complete the sentence. We ran out of the dorm, no one dared to touch the walls. We fell out into formation, in preparation of marching to the parade grounds, and finally graduation. During the graduation ceremonies, each flight is graded on timing of step, salute, return from salute, alignment, and a few other things. We did our DI proud. We got one of the highest marks for the day. That afternoon I was on a bus heading to San Antonio and Tech School. The discovery of the walls and what we did hung over our heads for the next week. Each passing week gave more relief than the previous week. After a couple of months went by, we figured that another flight would have gone through, adding a little more confusion as to which flight would have caused such havoc. As of this writing, the statute of limitations would be in effect and we could not be held liable.

Tech School

Not much to talk about while I was in Tech School. However, for some reason I got selected to be the guide-arm barer for the flight. This was a coveted position, rarely given to someone their first week and rarely to someone with less than ten weeks of tech school.   I was selected my first week and my tech school training was for eight weeks. Why was this such a coveted position? The greatest benefit was that guide arm bearers were able to be the first to enter the mess hall or cafeteria. This fact alone was worth the distinction. That first morning that I carried our flag of arms, I was really, really nervous. All I had to do was, on command, raise the flag straight up, second command, tilt the flag forward, third command, raise the flag up, forth command, lower the flag back to standard position. I made it. No mistakes, whew. As guide arm bearer, I have to carry the coat of arms where ever I go. To, class, to chow, even to bed, that is next to my bed. So, after we were dismissed, I carried the banner with me to class. Later that day, I was out in a courtyard were many of us congregate for lunch. While there, I met an airman that had been at tech school for a while, and just happen to be a guide arm bearer. We talked, and he was amazed that I was one as well, being this was my first week of school. Very quickly we struck up a friendship and he began to show me some of the tricks of the trade. Before I knew it, it was time to get back to class.

That evening, I fell into position, in preparation for our parade past the viewing stand. A little background.   Each flight is comprised of 100 airmen, 12 rows, eight per row. Two airmen are out front, one carrying the U.S. flag, the other, the Air Force flag. The guide arm bearer and the flight leader are two paces behind, the flight leader, front left and myself at front right. In total, there were about 25 flights. We started our march. We were getting closer and closer to the viewing stand where the generals, colonels and captains would stand in observation as we marched past. I was in a dilemma. Do I, or don't I? That was the question that went through my mind. What if I fail? The whole flight would lose points, meaning a lower number to get into the mess hall, meaning less time afterwards for personal stuff. Meaning a whole lot of guys are going to be angry if I mess up. Do I or don't I? Our flight leader gave the preparatory command to raise the banner. Fl-i-i-i-g-ht! The moment of truth. Do I or don't I? As I began to raise the banner or flag, I twirled the flag so that it went up in a rotating manner instead of straight up. Immediately, you could tell the impact on our flight. The steps were crisper, louder and when the flight leader called, "Pre-e-s-e-e-e-n-n-t Arms," all of our heads snapped as one. It was a beautiful thing. We could see the sharpness of our flight's action had an immediate impact on some of the people in the viewing stand. I suspect the impact was much greater on those who were witnessing the parade of flights for the first time. I held the flag high, and with pride. I could feel the instant respect from the guys. What I did was unheard of, for the first day with the flag; and yet already I made them feel proud. Once we passed the viewing stand, I didn't just lower the flag in a downward motion. When the flight leader gave the command, I reversed the motion that I used to raise the flag and twirled it into the down position. Again, a small but noticeable reaction from the flight. Yea man! Life was good. We ate early at the mess hall that evening.

I made through tech school without putting any holes in the walls and did very well in my classes. Thus far, the Air Force life wasn't too bad.

Seymour Johnson AFB

After Tech School and a short leave back in LA, I checked in at my first assignment, Seymour Johnson AFB, just outside of Goldsboro, NC. I sat down with the 1st Sergeant and he began asking me some questions.

"In high school did you play any sports, receive good grades, run for any office or participate in any other extra-curricular activity?"

"Yes, Sir. I was elected to a student body government position, was a member of Knights, a boy's club, dedicated to upholding the school's honor, lettered in swimming and football, plus some other clubs and activities. Oh, yes, I made the honor roll my senior year."

"He said, "Yea, I thought as much. I was looking over your entrance exam, do you know you scored 90 out of 95 in Electrical, Mechanical, and Math, and a 75 in Administration? And, 75 is high for a guy in Administration. Evidently you can type. Huumm, have you ever thought about applying for the Air Force Academy?"

"Uh, no sir I have not," was my reply. "I didn't have anyone that could coach me or help me decide my career, so the Air Force Academy never entered my mind as a possibility."

Little did I know that this conversation would one day save my life. The 1st sergeant wrapped up the meeting, welcomed me to the base and sent me on my way.

Since myself and another airman, Steve, who went to tech school with me, were the first to fill our new specialty, we had no one in charge of us. We had to inspect the F-4 fighters, B-52, KC-135, and other planes stationed at the base for corrosion, paint deterioration and metal fatigue. The B-52 is a unique aircraft. It was built in 1952, has seen action in Vietnam, the 1991 Gulf War and many of them are in active service today. The KC-135s look like a Boeing 707, but are supped up with the equivalent of a turbo-charger. As they are proceeding down the runway for take-off, water is dumped into the engine exhaust, still within the confines of the engine. The water turns to steams, expands violently and adds to the thrust. A 707 on steroids.

Steve and I were also in charge of the flight wash area. We would have Sergeants, Tech Sergeants, or Master Sergeants, who were crew chiefs, bring their F-4s to the wash area to get them cleaned up. Most people wouldn't think about it, but planes have to be washed too. It helps to keep dirt and other grime from building up. Anyhow, myself and Steve would supply all the equipment necessary to wash the planes, but it was up to the Sergeants, Tech, and Master Sergeants to do the actual washing. Now, we had one stripe on our sleeve, and yet, we were supervising sergeants that had 4-5 stripes.

In fact, one sergeant looked at our sleeve then looked at his sleeve, and said, "I think I joined the Air Force too soon."

It didn't take long before the word was out, that there were junior airmen supervising sergeants and other more senior airmen. But we didn't rub it in, and occasionally, we pitched in to help. Eventually I got to know a couple of civilians that worked on the base that worked in the adjacent paint shop. We worked there as well, but the "car wash" was our domain.

One day one of the civilians (I'll call his name Earl) who worked on base came up to me and said, "How would you like to come to my house, meet my wife and a few friends, and, of course have dinner?"
Dinner, now that sealed the deal. It doesn't take long of mess hall eating to where a person begins to long for a home cooked meal. That same week I went to Earl's home, and a few times thereafter. Earl, his wife and I got along really well and there were times when we just sat on the front porch and just talked. They were very interested in LA, and I showed as much interest in the country life. One day, about four or five of Earl's friends came over with their wives. The result was an impromptu party. Several of Earl's friends got to drinking, and Earl began to get concerned.

He approached one friend, whose name is Bill, and said, "Bill, you've had enough, why don't we go outside and talk a spell?"

"I don't want to talk to you, I want to talk to that little nigger over there."

The whole room got quiet. I told Earl that I would be leaving now, and I thanked him for the invite. Well Bill didn't leave enough alone. He followed me outside, and unbeknownst to any of us, Bill also had a knife in his possession. He quickly escalated his confrontational attitude to where he became belligerent. By now, everyone that was inside, now were outside. Bill was not listening to Earl, his wife or anyone else. Next thing I know, Bill pulled a knife and lunged at me. I spun around, back handed the knife hand away from me, continued the rotation, came up behind Bill and put him in a full nelson (arms underneath the armpit and back behind his neck). I forced Bill to bend until his head almost touched his knees. With continued pressure with my right hand on his neck, I let go of his left arm, and reached across and removed the knife from his right hand and pushed him away. The suddenness and potential violence of the incident was electrifying. I think everyone was in shock. Earl began to apologize profusely, and a couple other friends of Earl took Bill inside. I thanked Earl for the invite and went back to the base. I think Earl and much later, Bill was concerned about whether I would file a complaint and press charges. I didn't. I may have stopped by Earl's house only a couple of times after that incident.

There was a time in my life where Lucille Ball, of I Love Lucy fame, had nothing on me regarding clumsiness. One Friday afternoon Steve and I were in the shop doing small stuff to stay busy. We had no planes on the pad and none were scheduled. The first sergeant came by to check on his charges. Since Steve and I were the only ones with our specialty we had no one in which we reported, so the First Sergeant would occasionally stop by and spend some time with us. We shared the shop with about three or four other guys, but we had no association. When he walked in the shop, he saw that we were busy but had nothing on the schedule.

He walked around a few minutes, made small talk and then said, "How would you guys like to have the rest of the afternoon off?"

"No, way!"

"Oh yea!"

All six of us instantly went into high gear to get things cleaned up and ready for the next work day which would mean Monday. Which would mean leaving the base early, which would mean beating the traffic, which would mean getting to the city sooner. The shop has a cement floor that we regularly mopped and kept really clean. Well, I was cleaning, and moving, and pushing when I pushed a stack of paint cans closer to the wall. One of the paint cans had a lid that was not on very tight. It was aluminum paint. As I pushed the stack the aluminum paint can toppled. There was this sound that reverberated throughout the shop. Everyone stopped and turned in my direction, hoping for the best, expecting the worst. They got the worst. The noise was bad, the paint spilling out on the floor was worse still. At that moment, I don't think I had a friend in the shop. The rush to get outa Dodge was over. Without a word, we began to pick things up off the floor and put them on benches, cabinets, and tables. There was no way we were going to be able to clean that paint up without leaving some residue. We found two more cans of aluminum paint, popped the lid, and began painting the floor. We didn't leave early that afternoon.

I couldn't go to another episode without mentioning my friend, Charlie Brown. Not the cartoon character, but a real-life Charlie Brown. Sometimes we called him Mickey. He was from Richmond, VA, had a 1964 Ford Galaxy, bucket seats and four on the floor. We use to "cruise" the little town of Goldsboro a many of weekends. Mickey's family was well known in Richmond and he carried himself with confidence and had a little bit of cockiness about himself. Occasionally, on some weekends we would make the three-and-a-half-hour drive to Richmond to see his parents and some of his friends. I was only 18 at the time, so much of what we did was to attend parties or hang out at some of his friend's house. Wasn't interested in going to a bar or lounge anyway. I think some of the girls thought I was a little exotic, young, in the service, being from LA, talked with an accent (remember, I'm in the south), and my hanging out with Mickey didn't hurt. Anyhow it made for some interesting dates.

Some Friday or Saturday nights Mickey and I would come back from cruising, and would stop in at the Mess Hall for the midnight breakfast. Mickey weighed over 200 pounds and I weighed, at the time, about 160 pounds. The first time we went, he challenged me to an eating contest. I took him on. He and I got a tray and got in line. He started out with three pieces of bacon. I got four. He added two more pieces on his plate. I matched him. I got three eggs, hash browns, and three pancakes. Mickey matched me on ever item. We went and sat down. The word got out that a contest was in the making, David and Goliath.

We finished the meal and Mickey looked at me and said, "For a little guy you can eat a lot, but I matched you item for item."

I looked at Mickey and said, "Ready for seconds?"

The few airmen in the Mess Hall began to holler and shout and said they didn't believe that I could eat any more. I went back for seconds. Mickey didn't even get halfway through his second helping when he raised a white napkin indicating he was surrendering.

Seymour Johnson was a Strategic Air Command and a Tactical Air Command or SAC and TAC base. As I mentioned before, we had the big B-52 bombers and KC 135 tankers (see Fig. 9-1) for SAC and F-4s, F-100s, F101 fighters for TAC. One day I was walking across the tarmac when I got this strange and funny sensation on the back of my neck. I stopped and looked around. I didn't see anything out of the ordinary. Strange. The feeling wouldn't go away. I started walking again. I

Fig 9-1 B-52 about to be re-fueled by a KC135 Stratotanker

stopped looked around again. I don't know if you have ever seen a .50 caliber bullet. It is huge. It is about as big around as a thumb on an average sized man and longer than the middle finger. As I began to walk again, I kept turning my head to see if I can spot what was giving me this crazy sensation. Ah, ha. There it was, and, boy, I wished it wasn't. A set of quad 50's tracking me. Evidently, the weapons guys were testing the four rear guns on a B-52 and needed something to focus on. I was that something. I know I told you a .50 caliber is about as round as a person's thumb (see **Fig 9-2**), however, when it is pointing at you, somehow it seems like the size and diameter of exhaust pipes. Can you imagine, four of these monsters pointing at you? No wonder I got chills on the back of my neck (see **Fig. 9-3**). I learned to rely on that sensation several times in my tour with the Air Force. I spent about eleven months at Seymour Johnson before I got orders to ship out.

Just a few months prior to my shipping out, we got a Staff Sergeant in to take over the office. I guess the other sergeants felt a little envious of our position. Actually though, we knew the department was going to grow and it needed a more senior airman in charge. Still, we enjoyed our position while it lasted. Since our MOS (military occupational specialty) was new, and the sergeant coming in had no clue of what to do for our specialty, I was asked to train him. I sent a request from the tech school to get some training material and the exams. Fortunately, the school had just completed a six-month training curriculum and would rush the material to me. The course was in six parts, so I put the sergeant on a 30-day training period for each part. After the first exam, in which the sergeant got all but two answers correct, the First Sergeant called me and the sergeant into his office. "Did you administer an 'open book' exam?" He asked. "No, Sir. It was closed book." The next exam, the First Sergeant sent an observer to witness the administration of the test. The Sergeant got a perfect score.

The third test went the same way. During the middle of the third period, I got my orders to go overseas. I was able to complete the third course in training and administered the exam but could not start the fourth. My peer, Steve, was going to have to take over the training. While overseas, I got a letter from the sergeant indicating that his training didn't go too well upon my departure. On the next exam, under the tutelage of Steve, he got the equivalent

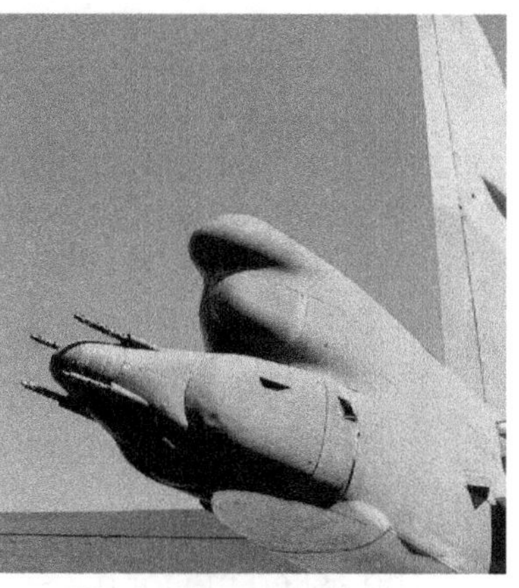

Fig 9-3 Quad .50 Caliber Machine Guns

of a low "C" and the First Sergeant wasn't very pleased. The First Sergeant said, "Airman King made this training thing look easy, evidently it is not. Let's put your training on hold, get Airman Steve trained to be a trainer, and pick up again later." I was pleased that they then realized the amount of effort I put in to gain the knowledge to be able to train someone else. But again, that was the beginning of my trademark, sometime to my detriment, "making the difficult look easy."

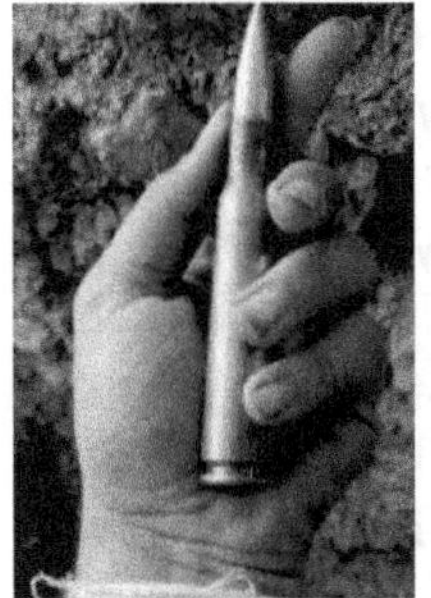

Fig 9-2
.50 Cal Bullet

Shipping Out

It was December, 1967 and I was in LA, enjoying the Christmas holiday with the family. I had my orders for Thailand and was to report to an Air Force Base just outside of San Francisco on 29 December. I had never been to San Fran, so I decided to report in a couple of days early, stay at the visiting airmen's quarter, and go into San Fran for a couple of days. I was too green to know that you can never expect the military to do what you think they will do. I reported in at the base about 10:00 PM on 27 December.

"Mel King, hmmm…that name seems familiar. Wait here, I'll be right back."
The sergeant was gone for about five to seven minutes.

"I thought so. You're on a priority listing. You'll be heading out on an eight o'clock flight."

"Wait a minute, I'm not supposed to even be here until 29 December!" I said.

"Problem is, you are here and I have my orders….'get you on the first available flight.' So, find yourself a place to hunker down, you're not leaving to go anywhere until I put you on that plane."

Now, why did I rate such a priority? I don't know.

"Are you sure you have the right King? I've only been in the service for a little over a year. Why would they be in a hurry for me?"

I tried to convince him that he had the wrong King, however, he asked me for my serial number, they matched.

"Oh well, San Fran, I'll see you another day," I said.

At 0600 hrs., I was escorted to the Mess Hall for breakfast, was on the plane by 0730 hrs., and in the air by 0800 hrs. Our first stop was Hawaii. Talk about a tease. Hawaii….and we have to stay in the airport. Many of the airmen on the plane with me were on their way to Vietnam. We were in a commercial Boeing 707 and I was one of just a few in the plane going to Thailand. At our stop-over in Hawaii, they let us off the plane while it was being serviced and refueled. It was about 11:00 AM, but on our time clock it was around 2:00 PM. We walked down the boarding ramp unto the hot, blistering tarmac. Since we were a military flight, we didn't pull up to a gate, therefore, we had about 100-yard walk to the terminal. With nothing much to do, as a group, we all decided to go to the bar to get a glass of beer. There may have been about 150 of us, with about a third being over 21. We never gave it a thought.

We went to the bar, filled the place up and ordered a round of beer for everyone. The waitress and bar tender said that they had to check IDs, and only those over 21 would be served. It wasn't three seconds before the mob, yes, in the blink of an eye the 150 of us transformed from joking, kidding, young kids to an unruly mob, a beast whose action could not be predicted. As one, even those over 21, considered the injustice of it all. We're on our way to Vietnam, ready to kill or be killed, and legally we couldn't have a beer. The boisterous attitude of us all rose very quickly and startled, no, frightened bartender and waitresses alike. I believe the rationale that all of us had was, so, put us in jail, it will either keep us from having to go or delay our going to Nam. Either one was acceptable.

Fortunately for the restaurant or us, I don't know which, there was an old (about 30 years old), veteran, seasoned sergeant that took command of the situation. He jumped on top of a table, and with a D.I. type of voice commanded everyone to be quiet. There was an immediate drop in decibel levels as everyone began turning their attention to the sergeant. He gave a short speech about how important each and everyone of our roles were to the war effort and we would be doing our country a disservice if we were detained or sent back home.

Somebody yelled out, "We can kill and be killed but can't drink beer, what disservice is that?"

The sarge said he had a solution and looked at the bartender in the eye and said, "Either this works, or I walk outa here."

The bartender knew the flames had not gone out, but that the kettle was just brewing. He looked around the room and I'm sure what he saw on the faces of all of us was, "any excuse will do," and the rioting would begin in earnest. The bartender looked at sarge and gave a slight nod.

Sarge said, "Gentlemen, here is what we are going to do. Now I know those of you over 21, made a long trek, out on that tarmac from the plane, to this here facility. And, I know that long trek made you mighty thirsty. I also know that in order to quince that thirst, you probably need at least three, maybe four bottles of beer, is that right?"

"YES SIR!"

One thing for certain, we weren't slow. Those that were over 21 dispersed themselves so that each table had at least one person over 21. It was a long, hot walk from the plane and it was amazing that the guys over 21 needed at least three bottles of beer to cool down.

Next stop was Midway Island. Not much happening here. You could get on a six-foot step ladder and see the whole Island. In fact, the highest point above sea level was about four feet. We didn't stay long, just enough to refuel and re-supply. Our next stop was Viet Nam.

We landed at the Air Base in Saigon and it's been about 18 hours of flying time since we started from Los Angeles. We disembarked from the plane and went to some bungalows where many of the other airmen would be spending the night. Most airmen on the plane would stay in-country while about 20 of us would continue on to Thailand. After about four hours, the twenty going to Thailand were marched over to a C-130 cargo plane and loaded up. No convenience here. Unlike the civilian plane, the seats didn't go back, not even a little bit, there was web seating and nothing associated with climate control. Another four hours that would seem like eight with the conditions we were sitting in. We finally arrived in Bangkok, at a civilian terminal. I was paired up with a Staff Sargent that was on his way back from R&R (Rest & Recuperation), had been in Thailand for about six months, was stationed at Udorn-Thani and was assigned to meet up with me to help get me to the base and registered.

I asked the sarge if he knew where the rest rooms were and he said sure, I'll take you. I walked into the restroom while he waited outside. There were two urinals and three stalls in this facility. One stall was being used. I proceed to the urinal and was standing there when I hear the toilet behind me flush and amazingly, a young Thai woman walks out, looks me in the eyes, and says, "Sawa dee kaa," and proceeds to wash her hands. I am still standing at the urinal. Understand I had a thousand things flash through my mind, am I in the wrong place, why is she here, if I move, a lot of this restroom is going to get wet, ..." I didn't know to zip up full stream or not. I shifted my body as much as I could to block her view, but I could feel my temperature rising. I am a red-blooded American male, 19, full of vim and vigor and I'm standing next to a woman (cute too) that I don't know, using the restroom. Shocking. It took her two days to wash her hands, at least it felt like it. After she left, I zipped up, washed my hands and hurried out before another female entered. As I walked out, the sarge was leaning against a tree, laughing so hard he couldn't stand up straight. I turned around to see if he purposely took me to a "Women's" restroom and set me up. After all, I could not read Thai so I wouldn't have any idea. But then I thought, there was a urinal in that restroom. As it turned out, the restroom had no markings, and in Thailand, that amounted to what we would call a unisex facility. Welcome to my first hour in Thailand. From there we went to the Airmen's quarters. I took a shower but just wasn't up to washing my hair (I mention this as it becomes a factor for another experience later). There were two reasons I didn't venture forth until the next morning when I would get on another C-130, take the final leg of the trip and fly to Udorn AFB, in northern Thailand, which was another two hours away. The first reason I didn't venture out again was, I was absolutely exhausted; the second, I didn't think that I could handle another cultural shock of the magnitude that I already experienced. Remember, I'm from South Central LA where San Fernando Valley and Orange County were about as foreign as it got. We are talking about major shock waves here.

I got up the next morning, performed my ablations and got on the plane with sarge. Once again, it was a C-130 cargo plane (see Fig. 10-1) with no windows. Since cargo didn't need to see, so, being cargo with no windows, I didn't see what the country side looked like. Still, I was excited to know my journey was coming to an end, so I thought.

Fig. 10-1 C-130 Hercules - Turboprop

We landed at Udorn-Thani AFB where I was checked in, assigned sleeping quarters and given the rest of the day off. The next day I would go through full registration and report for duty. The sarge was still playing big brother, and just so happened to be in the same barracks as I was in. We got on the base bus that would take us from the flight line to the living area. On the way I observed a couple, at least I thought they were a couple, where the woman was walking behind the man about three feet. I observed this more than a couple of times, and I thought, "strange." As we continued, I saw two men walking and they were walking arm in arm. I thought, "weird." Continuing further, I saw this arm in arm thing repeated. I turned to say something to Sarge, and all I saw was a big Cheshire cat grin on his face. I turned back to the window and never asked the question. I just thought to myself, "what more am I going to experience in this strange place, I am truly a 'Stranger in a Strange Land.'" Welcome to my first afternoon at Udorn AFB, Thailand.

First Day in Udorn Thani

At the barracks I was showed where I would be bunking and was introduced to the few guys that were there. The rest of the day was fairly uneventful. Then came the night. It was about an hour after sunset, most of the guys had returned from the mess hall and I was being introduced all around. Sarge was really taking great care of me, as long as I kept me out of the way of myself. After the intros, the guys started tending to their own personal affairs, and as far as they were concerned, I began to blend into the background. While I was getting organized it crossed my mind that I forgot to ask Sarge a question.

Sarge's bunk was a little distance away from mine so I was a little loud when I said, "Hey Sarge, I noticed when I came in from the Mess Hall that there was lightning and thunder on the horizon, does it rain here often?"

It got extremely quiet, everyone froze, and slowly, ever so slowly, everyone's head began to turn in my direction. I went from background to center stage in the blink of an eye. Suddenly, there was this outburst of laughter. I think Sarge was laughing the loudest and hardest.

After gaining a little composure, Sarge looked at me and said, "Airman, that isn't lightning and thunder, that's the noise and flashes of bombs going off. We are only 20 miles from Vientiane, the capital of Laos, it's where the Vietnam war originally started. Problem is, it's still continuing in Laos, it's just overshadowed by Vietnam."

Welcome to my fist night at Udorn, AFB.

The next morning, I didn't fare any better. I didn't have to go in as early as everyone else, but through the noise of everybody getting dressed and the excitement I had, I couldn't sleep, besides a rooster started crowing… and wouldn't you know it I had another bad attack of foot-n-mouth disease.

I said, to no one in particular, but rather loud, "Gee, that rooster sounds just like the one's back in the States!"

Once again it got quiet, once again the heads turned, and once again the laughter.

Someone shouted, "What, did you expect it to have, a Thai accent, like, clocka doodle dooole?" They laughed even harder.

Someone else said, "Hey, Sarge, you got any more like him, we can use a few more."

Welcome to my first morning at Udorn. And, it didn't end there. Sarge said that he had to go and check in but he will be back in an hour to collect me to go to registration. With that said, I collected my shaving kit, wrapped my towel around me and headed to the latrine. Since there were only guys in our part of the base, it was not uncommon to wrap a towel around you and off you went. The latrines were a separate bungalow connected by elevated, wooden walkways. I found out that the walkways were elevated due to the rains at monsoon season. There would be so much water on the ground that we would be walking in six inches of mud if not for the walkways. I found out much later, however, that we often didn't walk on the elevated walkways during the rains of monsoon season. Thailand, Vietnam, Cambodia and Laos have these snakes that are called, "Seven Steppers." Seven steps and you're dead. These snakes would often climb up on the walkways to get away from the water, so rather than argue with the snakes, we walked in the water instead. I entered the latrine and was surprised at how big it was. Everything was open, except the stalls for the toilets had sides but no doors. There were about 20 shower positions and I had my choice. I began to lather up.

Since Sarge was going to be back in an hour, I figured I had plenty of time to wash my hair. I had soap all over, hair, face, and body. I had my eyes closed and was just enjoying the shower when I heard the dreaded,

"Sawa dee kaa" in a high octave.

Oh nooo. Not again! This was even more embarrassing. Me in my birthday suit, sparsely adorned with soap. Not fair! The assault is too much. How much does a guy have to take? Soap be darned. I quickly rinsed off my head and face, grab my towel and ran out of the latrine into Sarge and other occupants of my bungalow. They were hollering. A total set-up. All the guys of every bungalow pitch in to hire a "cleaning lady" who comes around every morning to shine shoes, sweep the barracks, and CLEAN THE LATRINES. Sarge had timed his "leaving" to coincide with the arrival of the cleaning lady, knowing that I would take advantage of the hour that he would be gone. I was still red from the embarrassment and their laughter only caused me to turn a deeper shade.

One of the white guys, said, "Hey Sarge, I didn't know you black guys can turn red."

As with the comment this morning about the rooster and Thai accent, that didn't help matters at all.

Another airman said, "Sarge, we really, really like this guy."

I was all but 19 years old and my psyche was really taking a hit. I finally got dressed and Sarge and I went to go get me registered.

That evening, the guys from the barracks wanted to take me into town, Udorn-Thani. Going into town, being immersed in a higher concentration of Thai culture, humph, after today's experience I couldn't imagine what was waiting for or going to happen to me. But, if I was going to live with these guys, I couldn't say no. The town was about 10 klicks (kilometers, or about 6 miles) from the base, so we took the twenty-five-cent taxi ride (this is in December, 1967) into town and stopped at one of the favorite watering holes. It was a westernized bar with a bunch of GIs all

over the place and a few Thai women peppered around. The guys proceeded immediately to initiate me and ordered two bottles of beer. I rarely drank and especially didn't like beer. I forced down one bottle and carried the other with me. I started the acting, slurring my words and claiming that this place was unfair in that, I had so much happened to me and it's only been 24 hours. The guys began to re-tell the stories, the lightning, the rooster and especially the shower. Sarge wouldn't leave enough alone, of course he had to tell the story about what happened in Bangkok. Everybody was having so much fun at my expense. As the evening wore on, I guess it was night now, the guys tried to hook me up with one of the Thai girls that were in the bar.

She was small, very pretty, and had shapely legs. She also had this glean in her eye when she was told that I had just arrived and this was my first day in country. She got this predatory look. I feigned illness from drinking too much too soon, and said I think I needed to return to base. I didn't want to be in a bad state of mind on my first day on the job. And besides, I didn't know the girl. I had my scruples. Didn't matter. She grabbed hold of my arm and wouldn't let go. With all the attention focused in my direction, a couple of other Thai girls came over. They looked me up and down, said a few words in Thai to the girl holding my arm, and another grabbed my other arm. I felt helpless. I felt like a hen in the clutches of a fox, no several foxes. Of course, all the guys really thought this was funny, reveled in my discomfort, and provided no way to escape. But Sarge, oh yes, but Sarge came to my rescue. He suddenly realized that I was in his charge and if I reported in to work, especially the first day, halfcocked, he would be held accountable. So, he told the guys he didn't want me out of his sight.   There were the moans and groans from the guys, but no one argued with Sarge.

Once the girls realized that the prey could be looked upon and not taken, they too walked away, but turned back a couple of times as if to say, "Next time." I didn't know to shudder or smile. The first girl didn't turn away, but continued to hold my arm. The guys helped me with her name and I told her mine. She knew a little English and I knew no Thai. It was a little awkward. Soon afterwards, Sarge came over again and said that he had to get me back to base. Of course, everyone was telling Sarge that he could go, but leave the "newbie." Sarge laughed but continued to escort me from the bar, called a cab, and got me back to the base. That was my first night in the town of Udorn-Thani.

Udorn – Exile

I checked in to work the next day, and as before, I was one of two airmen that had the same Air Force Specialty Code (AFSC), or occupation. I'll take this time to tell you about Udorn, AFB, Just so you can appreciate the environment in which we worked. Udorn was the closest Air Force base to Hanoi, the capital of North Vietnam, and about 20 miles from Vientiane, the capital of Laos. Aircraft stationed at the base:

F-4 Phantom: Front line fighters that provided air cover and conducted bombing raids over Hanoi

F-105 Thunder Chief: Fighter bomber that had an internal bomb bay that could carry a nuclear warhead or about 2 tons of dumb bombs

F-106 Delta Dart: Base defense and Air to Air attack fighter

A-1 Skyraiders: Korean war vintage single prop fighter/ bomber that could carry one and a half times its own weight. Had unique capability of landing with bomb load if not expended

B-26 Marauder: Two engine prop bomber that could out fly and outperform most propeller driven fighters – WWII vintage

C-47 Skytrain: A two engine prop WWII vintage cargo plane

DHC-4 Caribou: A two engine prop WWII vintage cargo plane

C-123 Provider: A two engine prop Korean war vintage cargo plane

C-130 Hercules: A four engine Turbo-prop (jet engine driving the propellers) cargo aircraft

At check-in I was informed that I would be working 12-hour shifts, six days a week and although I may get shot at occasionally, there is no combat pay, since technically the war does not exist in Thailand. I just lo-o-o-ve politicians. I wonder if politicians think that bullets would know the difference between Vietnam and Thailand. Don't think so. It didn't take long to get into the routine of things. I went into town again a couple of times that first week. Something happened on one of those visits that completely altered the rest of my stay in Thailand. In spite of all that he did, Sarge and I were developing a close friendship. That first weekend he and I and a few other airmen went into town to hear this Thai band.   It was in a local park and one of the guys had a contact that permitted us to have close up seats during the performance. The voices were amazing as the group sang some of the most popular songs of the time, sounding very much like the original artists. One of the singers really got my attention. I started winking, smiling and acting foolish, as most airmen do, to get her attention. She completely ignored me. As the band was getting close to finishing their set, I blow her a kiss. Ah-ha, I saw a brief smile. My hope climbed a million stairs. Once I got the smile from her, I then began to ignore her. Now it was her turn to try to get my attention. I played hard to get.

After the set was over, we went backstage (don't know how, but we did) and I had a chance to meet this … this, China doll from Thailand. Sarge looked at me, looked at the singer, the chemistry was obvious. Problem was, she spoke very little English and I spoke no Thai. Frustration. I reached for her hand, and without saying a word, we left the others and just walked through the park. No words were spoken. We just walked. After a short period, we returned back to the group. I kissed her on the cheek, turned to Sarge and said, "I'm ready to go." I knew I would never see China doll again. But it was so nice to meet a young lady, not in a bar, who was not willing to do whatever for just a few dollars. One of the amazing things about this encounter was the singing group themselves. The group was singing popular American songs, note for note, word for word…but, they themselves couldn't speak English, none, nada, nothing. So, when I first started talking to China doll, and she pretended she didn't understand (at least I thought she was pretending) I figured she was paying me back because of my ignoring her earlier. I was stupefied. The clarity of their singing, in English, and yet they did not understand the language. Amazing.

After meeting the group and my return with China doll from the brief walk in the park we all decided to leave. I was very down and disappointed as a result of my experience with China Doll, so, as I mentioned before, I was ready to go back to the base. Sarge and the rest, however, were not ready to go back, and I was too new to the country to chance or risk it on my own. Occasionally, a few airmen would come up missing from their trek into town. No where to be found. We were given that stern warning when I checked in. Always, always travel with two or more. So, I had to tag along with the guys while we/ they went bar hopping. We eventually made it to one of the favorite spots, and the guys settled down for some serious socializing. The girls there some the guys knew, some were fresh faces. The guys began to pair up with the girls and began to excuse themselves one by one. I kept the table reserved as each of the guys would wander off and then return sometime later. They kept trying to introduce me to a couple of the girls, I just wasn't interested. I didn't like "picking" up a girl at a bar, I didn't like the fact that there was no relationship, and I didn't like the fact that it resulted in a "transaction." And besides, China doll was still on my mind. That night I made a vow. I would not come back into town to meet any girl until I could speak the language and meet and get acquainted with the Thai women as I would back in the states. I was going into a self-imposed exile. After I said that, I thought, Gee, I'm going to be here a year. It could be a long time before I come back if I don't learn the language. I better get started, and started quick.

Learning the Language

One of the peculiar things about Udorn, AFB is that the U.S. Government made an agreement with the Thai Government about having civilians work on base. The Thais are excellent craftsmen and so it was natural to have a large number in the shop that I was in. We monitored cracks and corrosion on all of the planes, but we were responsible for painting them as well. The day after my vow, I went to a couple of the Thai men and told them that I wanted to learn to speak Thai and that I didn't want them to speak English to me. They agreed to take on the task. It so happened that I was a fast learner as they often said. What they didn't know was that I was highly motivated. I didn't socialize well with guys at the time. I would have two or three good buddies, but the girls, numbers didn't matter, I was very relaxed talking with the gals.

One day, another one of those cultural surprises snuck up on me. As I learned to speak Thai from the two who volunteered to teach me, I began to communicate with the other Thais as well. As not too many GIs attempted to learn their language, they thought this was exceptional. To show their appreciation they accepted me into their society on base. This meant that if I was walking someplace and one of the Thais saw me, he would come along side and place his arm around my waist. Yep, my waist and walk with me. I did everything I could to keep from squirming. I recognized the honor given, but it was very, very uncomfortable. I told them that in the U.S., guys would sometimes put their arms around a buddy's shoulder, but never, never their waist. They would look at me as if I just told them a fascinating story, shrug, and continue to put their arm around my waist. And yep, you guessed it. When other airmen would see us walking, you can imagine the ribbing I got.

On another day, when I had time off, and on my self-imposed exile to base, I realized how much Thai I was learning. I was in one of the little deli's that Thais work in that was interspersed throughout the base. Two Thais were behind the counter cooking hamburgers, hotdogs and other items. There were two airmen ahead of me placing their order. Once the two Airmen placed their order with the Thai at the counter, the Thai at the counter called back to the other cook to prepare the Airmen's order. Problem was, the Thai also said something else.

When I heard what he said, in English, I said, "I think you owe these guys an apology."

"Why do I owe them an apology?" The Thai at the counter said.

"Because I heard what you said."
The two airmen looked at me in puzzlement.

"What did he say?" The two Airmen asked.

"All I did was to call in their order." Said the Thai.

Without turning to look at the airmen, but my eyes locked on the Thai, I said, "He called you a dogface."
The Thai insisted that he said nothing wrong. In Thailand, as you might guess, being called a dogface is a very derogatory title.

The airmen obviously got very upset and threaten to have the Thai fired. I asked the airmen that if I got the Thai to apologize and no charge for their meal, would that suffice? They grumbled a little and then agreed. I turned to the two Thais, and speaking to them in Thai, explained the proposition. They readily agreed and call me a "number nung" or number one GI. Which is a good thing. From that day forward, the two Thais and I became friends. I was amazed at my pace for learning Thai.

After about two months, I decided that I would venture into town with the other guys in the barracks. None of them knew that I was learning Thai, so I thought I would see what would develop on this excursion and the breaking of my self-imposed exile. Of course, the guys all wanted to visit their favorite night spots. The girls were there, liquor was flowing and the music was loud. It didn't matter that the music was loud since not a lot of conversation was happening anyway. The language barrier was huge. The bar was not unlike many a bar here in the United States. There was the typical bar, stools, and a seating area with about seven or eight tables, four chairs to a table. I sat at one of the tables with the guys as they looked around the room for their favorite "gal."

It was up to the girls to have any GI, that they are sitting with, spend money on a few glasses of liquor before any of them would agree to leave the table with a GI and disappear. This process could take a couple of hours before the girls would get a signal from the bartender that it was OK to take the GI by the hand and leave the common area. Some of the guys who have been in country for awhile knew the system and would pay a few more bucks up front to accelerate the process. Oh, I forgot to say that Sarge was with us that night. The evening wore on and I was just enjoying being off base, being with the guys, and it didn't hurt that the girls were cute. But still, I couldn't see myself making a "transaction." Most of the guys were at the table when I got up enough courage to speak to one of the girls in Thai.

I said in Thai, "I apologized for not showing interest, that they were *"sway mock, poo-ying,"* (very pretty girls) that I felt uncomfortable in this type of surrounding, and did any one of them have a sister or cousin that I would be able to meet away from here?"

Everyone at the table stopped talking. They all looked at me, totally surprised. Then everyone began talking at once. The guys were asking what did I say? The gals began giggling, left the guys they were with and just piled up on me. Whoa, way too much happening and way too fast. Once again, I shattered the myth about black guys not turning red.

The guys began to laugh at my embarrassment and said, "Sarge, he hasn't lost his touch, we do like this guy."

I eventually crawled out of my predicament, but now, I was getting way more attention than I wanted. After a short while, it became very apparent what my role would be... I became the de-facto interpreter. Conversations became much livelier, and the guys began to see the gals as a person and started to really enjoy themselves. I botched some of the translation which only added to the laughter from the girls, which caused the guys to laugh more, which caused me to turn red more. As we were leaving, we all were invited back at the pleasure of the house. It turned out to be a great evening.

As my conversational Thai continued to improve, I first was invited to the homes of Thais that worked on base. It was great to see and feel the culture first hand. There were times when I would be eating with a family (I never asked what I was eating), when some kind of bug would show up on the plate. Not to offend or to embarrass, I would discretely, move the bug to one side and pray that there wasn't a second bug. Not so much that there was a second bug, but one that I didn't see. I got to enjoy the various meals, very different, but tasty in their own way.   More so, I took advantage of these invites to meet friends and relatives. It wasn't long, after the invite from the Thais on base that I began to branch out and meet Thais on my own.

Finally, one day, I was going on a date. For the sake of simplicity, I'll call her Sue. I met Sue at the park. She was sitting down reading a book and feeding pigeons (by the way, these pigeons sounded the same as the ones in, say New York - just for you smarty pants). I first greeted her in English to see what kind of response I would get. She looked up, saw that I was a GI, mumbled something under her breath and continued reading. I then greeted her in Thai and asked what she was reading. That got a little more response from her, but I could tell she was still wary. Us GI's have this ugly reputation of being girl chasers and expecting that money can buy anything. I'm sure she was thinking that somewhere in this conversation that I was going to see if she would consummate a "transaction." But I spoke to her in Thai and most Gi's don't speak Thai, so I know that added some confusion, possibly intrigue, to her thinking. I said something else to her, she laughed. She saw that I was not going away very easily, so she finally put her book down and began to pay attention. After a couple of times meeting Sue at the park, she agreed to go to the show. We saw a Bruce Lee movie and a few others. The strangest was Amos & Andy. Can you imagine Amos & Andy speaking Thai with a Southern drawl? From this encounter, I met others girls and I was invited to several "gatherings," town events and a number of events where I was the only GI present. My list of people that I knew grew fairly long. In fact, there were a couple of Thai guys on base who began to see me in town quite a bit, and at various locations. They were so intrigued by my association with so many different girls that they asked me if I could introduce them to a couple. I had to chuckle at that. With that request, I felt I accomplished what I sat out to do… meet girls in a non-bar setting and get to know them as a person.

You may not have given it much thought, but in order to do what I did, that is to learn about the Thai custom and their people, I often violated one of the base rules, "Don't travel alone."   On one occasion I had been invited to a couple's house who kind of adopted me. I would spend a lot of time there, meeting their family and just enjoying the friendship. Let me digress for a moment to talk about their home. The house was about 10 feet up in the air, on stilts. This was necessary due to the monsoons. When the rains come, the common mode of transportation is a canoe or a small boat of some kind. But because of the height and difficulty in climbing, I often wonder how some of the men could climb the steps or rather stairs when they come back from one of the men gatherings. The gatherings can be wild sometimes, but to keep this "G" rated, I won't go into detail.

One morning, after spending the night with my adopted family, I was walking back to base but had no idea where I was. This was the first time I had spent the night with them and the first time that I was leaving on my own. As I began walking it was soon apparent that I didn't know in which direction to go. I walked a couple of more blocks and saw and elderly man, bending down and tending a garden. His back was to me.

In Thais, I asked, "How do I get to town from here?

Without looking up, he pointed and told me directions.

I thanked him, "Kop koon" I said, and started walking away.

Out the corner of my eye, I saw him look up to see who he was talking to. He looked at me, saw a GI, looked the other way and didn't see a Thai.

In Thai he yelled, "Delcon, Delcon" or wait a minute. "Did you just ask me for directions?"

"Yes, that was me." I responded."

He then said, "Number 'nung' GI." (Number one, GI). Then he said in American, (the Thais in the area said they spoke "American" not English) "We are very close to the border (Laos) and it is not good for a GI to be out this way alone. Because you are number one GI, I will walk with you, keep you safe. Nobody bother you if I walk with you."

We walked, and talked, and laughed, (I still mispronounced or misused words) for what must have been about a half mile before we got to an area where a taxi would come. He stayed with me until I got in the cab.

Flight Line Operations

My work assignment or Air Force Specialty Code (AFSC) had me out on the flight line most of the day. I saw first hand some of the damaged planes returning from Vietnam and participated in assessing their flight worthiness. Being the closest Air Force base to Hanoi, we saw a lot of planes land at our base for repair. If they were too badly damaged, we would use them for their parts and cannibalize them. If badly damaged but salvageable we would route them to our Remote Area Maintenance (RAM) team. The RAM team could do wonders with an aircraft. Sometimes planes would have so many borrowed parts that Planes that I thought would never see the light of day, would find themselves flying. This cannibalizing made it tough to do real maintenance on the plane though. During routine maintenance of one of the RAM team's repaired aircraft, regular replacement parts rarely fit. So, we in turn had to modify the genuine replacement part to fit the altered part. You could do this only so many times until nothing would fit. It was amazing that these planes even flew. But fly they did.

Because of our close proximity to Vietnam, we often were targets of the Pathot Lao (locals friendly to the Vietnam cause) and these individuals would take shots at those of us on the flight line. This was a real danger to us, especially if we were on top of an aircraft with no interference or other obstruction to hinder a clean shot at us. Even without occasionally being shot at, the flight line was still a busy, hectic and dangerous place. Many of the safety rules that exist at stateside bases did not exist here. Often, we would climb on top of planes, 20 – 30 ft off the ground, with no safety harness, ladders or anything else between us and the ground. During a certain time of the year, we were cautioned to always hold on with one hand. Thailand has these huge beetles called, Rice Bugs. They were about three inches long with mandibles about half their length. One day I found out why I was told to always hold on with one hand. You see Rice Bugs fly…but they don't land very good. Also, I don't think they have gears. Once they get up to speed and are flying, they fly at a constant speed. Well, this one day I was on top of one of the planes, doing my job, minding my own business, totally engrossed. I had just completed inspection of a section of the plane, and since I was just beginning to stand up, I was not holding onto anything. Wham! I got hit in the back. I even felt blood trickling down my back. Oh my God, I've been shot! I was knocked down and laid spread eagle on the plane. When other airmen saw the way that I went down, everybody looked around to see if they could see or hear the source of the shot. Nothing. They came running over to see how I was.

I asked, "How bad is it?"

"Oh, I think it will survive." One of the Airmen said.

"It? What do you mean it?" I asked.

Everybody started laughing. As it turned out, one of those damnable rice bugs flew into me. The "blood" I felt was the darn bug walking down my back. I wanted to kill 'em, every last one of 'em. The dumb little creature.   Need I say what the talk of the barracks was that night?

As I mentioned before, Rice Bugs have one speed. They don't slow down to land. Every landing with them is a crash landing.   It's really humorous to watch.   If the bugs don't find an innocent victim working on a plane, they descend lower and lower to the ground, like an airplane  coming in for a landing. Upon contact with the ground, they will tumble over and over; and, if they land on their back, they'll open their wings to turn themselves over, shake a little bit, then walk off as if nothing happened. Dumb little creatures. Now that these rice bugs got my attention, from my previous encounter, I started paying attention to the Thais that worked on the base and how they were collecting them.   The Thais would essentially have one of those old-fashioned picnic baskets that have flaps that open on either end. Well, the Thais would wait for one of the bugs to come in for a landing, or crash into an innocent victim, run over to the bug and strangely, smell the bug. Some bugs they would keep; others they would put back on the ground. They would repeat this process until the basket was full. Soon I lost interest in those dumb bugs, until I realized that the Thais were out working the fields for these things for quite a while. I thought to myself, "Gosh they should be getting hungry and thirsty about now." No sooner had I made that thought that one of the Thais reached into her basket, smelled the bug again, bit its head off and began sucking the insides. It's quite logical really. The bugs eat the rice so the people eat the bugs. With the size of the mandibles on the Rice Bugs, I often wondered who took the first bite.   No, I never tried eating one.

The Shack – Emergency Landings

My work on the flight line began to gain some attention from a few senior sergeants and officers; and, as a result, I was assigned to head up a ancillary location with a few Thais assigned with me. The fact that I was starting to

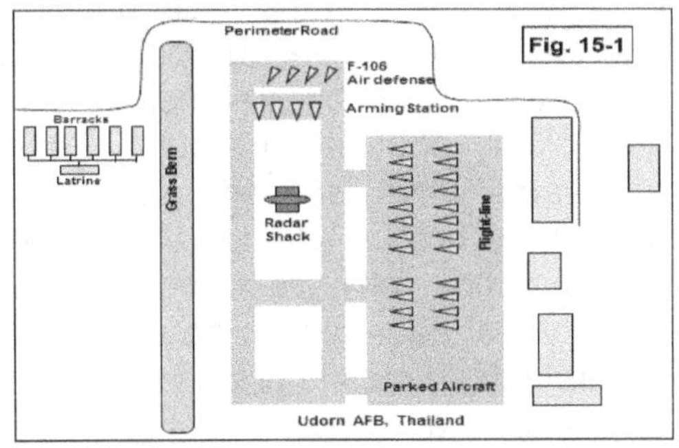

speak Thai was noticed by senior officers   and was one of the reasons they assigned me to the position. While in this location, we had an excellent view of the runway, and as a side benefit, many of the emergency landings. The Shack, as we all called the building that sat between the runway and taxiway, and housed the base air defense, was strategically place to be in a very eventful location (see **Fig. 15-1**). As planes would taxi to the arming location, each plane would turn and face toward the length of the runway and coincidentally towar d The Shack. Multiple times during the day, F-4 Fighter jets (see **Fig. 15-2**) would taxi to the arming station prior to take-off. The planes are loaded with bombs and missiles on the flight line, with pins in place, and then the pilot would taxi the plane over to the arming station. Missiles and bombs that are loaded on a plane have a "safety pin" in place to prevent accidental detonation. These pins have about an 18 X 2-inch tag hanging on them for visibility.   At the arming station, there would be several airmen that would go to each plane and pull the safety pins and arm each weapon just prior to take off. One particular day, four F-4 Phantoms were at the arming station having the safety pins removed.

F-4's are a formidable aircraft. They can carry a greater bomb load than a B-17 of WWII era, plus four Sparrow and two Sidewinder missiles, fuel tanks and ammunition for a 30 mm Gatling gun. One day as four of the F-4's were lined up at the arming station, facing toward The Shack, to have their safety pins removed, Sparrow missiles on one of the planes began igniting and firing off the plane. When the first missile went, it hit in front of the shack, a pause, the second hit to the side of the shack, a pause. In between the first and second missile, airmen inside began bailing out windows on the back of the shack. The third missile flew between the radar and the building, reached escape velocity and flew off the base to land in a field a few miles away. The fourth also landed in front of the shack. Later that evening we got together with the airmen from the shack and we all laughed and joked about the "bailout." Serious at the time, but funny afterwards when we began describing and talking about their "bailout" technique. Some head first, some straddled, some made an attempt but fell back inside. We had a great time. Their beers were on us that night. Little did they know that they would have several other times to practice "bailout" in the near future.

On a non-eventful day, a C-130, a four engine cargo aircraft, (see **Fig. 10-1**) was coming in for a routine landing with no indication of a problem. It circled the base once then went out to get on

Fig. 15-2

the approach pattern. Routine. No one paid any particular attention. It approached the base. Made it's final decent. Flared, touched the runway as smoke from the tires began billowing out from underneath. Routine. In order to shorten the length of runway needed to stop, many of the cargo planes will perform what is called "reverse thrust." Individual blades on the engine will actually rotate so instead of pulling air and pushing it over the wings, the blades will reverse the direction of air and push against the on-coming airflow, slowing the plane down. The pilot of this C-130 coasted a brief moment, then went into reverse thrust. Routine. What happened next was not routine. Two of the engines on one side of the aircraft went into reverse thrust mode, the two engines on the other side did not, they continued in their normal mode of operation. One side was pushing, the other side was pulling. The result immediately sent the C-130 into a spin, leaving the runway, and careening down the field, heading for the one building in-between the runway and taxiway, the Shack. Bailout. Once again airmen began running out doors and crawling out windows of the Shack with a remarkable improvement in form. The military has what we call a "pucker factor." It's when a person can be scared and their butt is so tight that they could pick up a piece of paper. As the C-130 was approaching the Shack, I'm sure the pucker factor of the pilots began to rise.

It's uncanny how, when something unusual happens, without a word spoken, it gets the attention of the whole flight line. All work ceased. The C-130 came closer and closer to the Shack, and slower and slower it moved as the pilot in their frenetic effort to stop the aircraft went to normal mode, eliminating the spin, and applied full brakes. Will it stop in time? Moreover, to add to the drama, when it was spinning, tires on the C-130 began smoking, and as it left the runway, it began to kick up a cloud of dust, occasionally obscuring it from view. We all held our breath. When the smoke cleared and the dust settled, the nose of the C-130 stopped 10 feet from the Shack. There was a loud shout up and down the flight line when it became apparent that both the C-130 and the Shack survived. Ten feet is not much of a margin when you consider the size of this aircraft. We met the guys from the Shack again that night and began ribbing them on how much their "bailout" had improved since the last time.

The Shack continued to have its moments. One other incident involving the Shack was with a Korean War vintage aircraft, called an A1A Skyraider (see **Fig 15 – 3**). It is

propeller driven, can carry its own weight in bombs and rockets, and unlike jets that can loiter only for about 30 minutes, this aircraft could loiter for a couple of hours to provide air coverage for troops on the ground. Also, the A-1, because of its slow landing speed, is one of the few aircrafts that can return from a mission and retain its bomb load. All other aircraft have to go to a bombing range to drop their ordinance prior to landing. An A-1 coming in for a landing, when compared to jets, is going so slow that it looks like it will fall out of the sky. But it is a steady aircraft, can take a lot of battle damage and is equal to if not better than the F-4 in survivability. And, true enough, it landed with no incident until it turned off the runway unto the crossway, right behind the Shack. As I mentioned, the A-1 can land with a full bomb load. Although it had dropped some ordinance, It still had two, one thousand pound bombs hanging under each wing when it landed. As it turned off the runway, one of its landing gears collapsed. This caused the weight of the plane to drive the bomb hanging under the wing to go through the wing itself and lodge there. The guys in the Shack monitor radio communications between the pilots and the tower, so when the pilot radioed an emergency, described what happened and stated his location…right behind the Shack…bailout. Once again, the airmen in the Shack performed egress in many different ways, but all done rapidly.

Flight Line – Emergency Landings

Daily, there was continuing excitement, some days more than others. The highlights were always when the siren would go off, indicating that we have an aircraft coming in from Vietnam with battle damage. Of the two primary fighters, the F-4 and the F-105, the F-105 was always the more exciting to watch. This day, for the first time, I was going to witness an emergency landing, an F-4. If a pilot had to crash an airplane, the plane of choice would be the F-4, hands down (see **Fig. 16-1**). It has several features that help to make it a very survivable aircraft. For instance, there is a pocket just above the left engine that houses an air turbine. If the F-4 loses it engines (it has two) and can't do a restart, then this turbine would pop up, air would cause propellers to spin and provide emergency electrical power until it reaches a certain airspeed. Once it reaches a set airspeed, the turbine switches from providing electrical power to providing hydraulic power so that the pilot will have control of the flaps, aileron, and rudder. Unfortunately, it is unable to provide enough power to lower the landing gears. However, with hydraulics available it will prevent the pilot from having to do what is called a "dead stick" landing. Landing without hydraulics would be like driving your car, no a truck, without power steering and would be extremely difficult to maneuver. Also, the F-4 is not shaped like a commercial liner, a cigar with wings but is a low-wing, flat belly aircraft. The fire trucks came out, we watched them spread foam on the runway, and waited. The foam does several things, it is a fire suppressant, is very slippery, and acts as a barrier. The F-4 made its approach, floated above the runway for about a quarter of its length, then sat down on the foam. It seemed to float on the foam and slid for about the length of two football fields. It didn't veer off the runway, didn't wiggle back and forth, and it didn't even turn sideways. A very "safe" emergency landing. We saw many F-4s come in for emergency landings, and they all did the same. Very uneventful. After awhile, when an F-4 declared an emergency, it barely got attention they were so routine.

The F-105 is a high wing aircraft (See **Fig. 16-2**). It has the characteristic cigar shape with wings. The landing struts are about 7 ft. long as compared to 4 ft.

of the F-4.   The shape of the F-105 made it such that it didn't handle crash landings very well. If the long landing gear collapses during an emergency landing, as they often do, it puts tremendous forces against the wing, causing it to break off, inducing a roll or tumble to the fuselage. Not good for the pilot. For this reason, whenever it is announced that an F-105 was coming in for an emergency, the whole flight line will turn out to watch. On one clear and bright sunny day, I was in the barracks when the word was passed that an F105 had declared an emergency. The barracks emptied immediately and all of us ran to the grassy knoll to get a good look at the landing. The knoll is a mound of dirt about 10 feet high, covered with grass, that runs alongside the runway to protect the barracks and living area from engine noise and debris from any explosion on the flight line or runway.

So, it was with a lot of excitement when it was announced that an F-105 was coming in for a landing and had declared an emergency. We waited in anticipation. We scanned the skies for several minutes when one airman, who had binoculars, yelled out, "There it is!" and pointed with his finger. There were about 40 – 50 of us on the knoll, and as one, we all turned to face in the direction he pointed. It was but a short time later when the airman with the binoculars looked as if he saw a ghost and began running away from the Knoll. Many of the airman stayed on the knoll, asking, "Why is he running? Not me. When I was growing up with the "crew," we saw too many movies where this one guy is asking, "Why is everybody running?" Then he turns around and what everybody was running from is right there and gobbles him up. So, it just became natural, when one of us started running we all did.

It was only as we were running would we ask the question, "Now why am I running?" It's amazing how quickly learned behavior kicks in. As we were running away from the knoll, I asked the airman, "Why are we running?" He was still too frightened to talk. It didn't take us long to get to a more distant and safer location where we could still see the runway.

Soon, we heard this loud shout "Run!" from those that remained on the knoll. As the F105 got closer, those on the knoll began to see with the naked eye what the other airman saw with binoculars. The F-105 had an unexploded Surface to Air Missile (SAM) stuck in its tail pipe. These missiles are also known as "Flying Telephone Poles," due to their similarity in thickness and height. In this instance, most of the missile had broken off and only about a six-foot section remained. However, that which remained was in direct line of the exhaust coming from the aircraft. It was amazing that the exhaust plume did not cause the missile to detonate. Where all of us were standing on the knoll was just about in line where the F-105 would touch down. Of course, we didn't know if the landing would jar the missile, causing it to explode, or fall out of the aircraft, hit the ground and then explode. In either case, on top of the knoll was not a good place to be. The plane touched down about as gentle as I have ever seen a landing, rolled, and with brakes only (he didn't use reverse thrust to slow down), it came to a stop. The Pilot opened the cockpit, un-strapped, crawled over the side, hung onto the edge of the cockpit, and dropped the remaining five feet to the runway. His feet no sooner touched the runway that he was in a full sprint to get behind the "Shack." I'm sure he would have set a world record in the 200-meter dash that day.

Warehouse Duty and nomination for Airman of the Month

Due to personnel shortage on the base, it was not uncommon for airmen to be loaned to another function. I got assigned, for about two - three weeks, to a warehouse unit. I enjoyed the work, and evidently it showed. The Warehouse commander had received a report on my work, and unbeknownst to me, came out to witness my efforts first hand. This report got back to my unit commander. I was not aware that my commander was already considering nominating me for "Airman of the Month" and the report from the warehouse commander sealed the nomination.   While I was at the warehouse things became fairly routine, except for this one afternoon. An airman on a forklift knocked over one of the oxygen bottles and the neck broke off. Whoa boy! That thing took off like a bat out of hell (who said bats were dumb, who'd want to stay in hell). That bottle put a hole in the warehouse wall, went through both walls of the adjacent building, careened off a stack of crates, elevated to a near vertical position and launched itself skyward. Wow! That was something to see.

While working at the warehouse I uncovered some documents that revealed one of the reasons why we were in Vietnam. Off the coast of Vietnam, there are several huge oil reserves; and naturally, the U.S. had an interest in protecting these resources.

Near the end of my working with the warehouse group, my commander called me to his office and briefed me on the Airman of the Month competition. After the briefing, I asked him when do I have to be there and where do I have to go?

His reply was "Now and in the General's office," and in that order.

I stood there stunned. No study, no rehearsal, nada.

"What are you waiting for airman?" the Colonel said with a grin.

I ran as fast as I could, with some compromise due to the humidity. It wouldn't do any good to appear in front of the General, and his staff, disheveled, sweaty and musty. I arrived at the General's office just as another airman was walking out. The attendant told me to wait a few moments to let the review team make their comments on the previous candidate, and then I will be asked to come in. I didn't have long to wait. I wouldn't have minded if they took all day. Can you imagine a 19-year-old standing in front of a General and four of his staff members? I tried to keep from sweating bullets. The moment of entry came all too soon. I entered the room and it was not only the General and his staff, but another visiting General was in the room. Oh boy. I went before the review team and began to answer their questions. Fortunately, I like to read and keep up with current events. They threw a lot of questions at me. I think though that there was one response that made the most impact. The visiting General asked me about a new member of the leadership that just arrived in

Vietnam. The General misstated his name. I informed the General on the correct pronunciation of his name (with snickers from the others) and proceeded to say what his role and objectives were. I was dismissed. I went back to my commander to debrief him. He was mildly attentive until I told him I corrected the General. With that comment he sat up in his chair, leaned forward and said,

"Tell me again what you did."

"Well, there was this visiting General and he asked me about the new leadership that arrived in Vietnam recently. He mispronounced the leader's name, and I corrected him."

He said, "Well you can kiss that award good-bye."

The Colonel was a decent officer and I felt badly that I disappointed him and let him down. Of all the airmen in his command, I was honored that he selected me. After all, there are only 12 per year that are selected from the entire base population. With a heavy heart I left his office and went back to the warehouse area. I only had a couple of days remaining with them.

I finished my assignment with the warehouse group and went back to my command. The first day I returned, the Colonel called me to his office. The guys that I was working took notice.

"You really have been called into the Colonel's office a lot lately, what kind of trouble you been getting into?" They asked.

Someone must have seen me enter the Colonel's office the two times for the Airman of the Month nomination. Since I was on temporary assignment at the warehouse, I never had an opportunity to talk with the guys in the shop to tell them what was happening. And besides, I didn't want to tell them about my latest, major goof up, correcting a General. Off I go, running once again. As I got close to the Colonel's office, I spotted him just as he spotted me. He had his hands on his hips and had about as much of a scowl that I had ever seen on his face. I began to dread what would come next. I began imagining a month of KP (Kitchen Police, aka, dishwashing) duty, latrine duty or guarding the trash dumpster (the latter, an obvious and meaningless chore). I approached him, stopped, saluted, and stood at attention. He stared at me for a few seconds.

Then he said, "Come in airman."

Bad trouble. At home you do something bad and your mom or dad will use every name you got. In the service, they leave out your name. They reduce you to a commodity. To be used and tossed away. I followed him into his office and stood at attention.

He said, "This may take awhile so sit down. I got the report back from the General and his staff of your actions at the Airman of the Month review."

He waited a few seconds.

"You won! They were impressed with your knowledge of current events and thought your correcting the General was ballsy, just what they want in leadership. Not only that, they have selected you to represent the base for 'Airman of the Year' at an upcoming contest to be held in the Philippines."

I sat stunned; as I am sure the Colonel did when he originally got the message. "Congratulations, Airman King." He said. I got my name back.

A car accident was announced today. If you recall, during the time of my self-imposed exile I made the following comment, "At check-in I was informed that I would be working 12-hour shifts, six days a week and although I may get shot at occasionally, there is no combat pay, since technically the war does not exist in Thailand." I just lo-o-o-o-ve politicians. Because we were technically not at war, any airman that was killed in combat, the press release said that they died in a "car accident." We had a number of car accidents throughout my stay. I was almost involved in one myself.

Orders

It was one of the few instances when I can at least remember the month when something happened while I was stationed in Thailand. It happened in April and once again I was called to the Commander's office. If you recall, at my first assignment out of Tech School, Seymour Johnson AFB, the First Sergeant, as a result of my Air Force entry scores, asked if I had ever thought about entering the Air Force Academy. My response to his question was that I had not given it any thought and was unaware that I would even qualify. Well, that First Sergeant never said what he was going to do, he just asked if I ever considered applying. Unbeknownst to me, he wrote up the papers and submitted my name as a candidate. What I received at this moment were orders to go to the Philippines. There I was to take a full physical and mental exam to see if I was physically and mentally sound. The results would determine if I would be admitted to the Air Force Academy. I was to head out the next day.

The following morning, I got on a C-130, again, and flew into Saigon. With duffle bag in hand, I walked to the Military side of the airport, entered the terminal and looked around for seating. The terminal was not very big and there was not a lot of seating. I didn't pay much attention when another airman came and sat across from me. I was in deep reverie as I pondered the hole in the ceiling, seeing the shaft of sunlight coming through, exposing the dust that was in the air. Just two days before, a mortar round came through the ceiling, exploded, and killed an airman named Sam. He had just finished his tour of duty and was sitting not far from where I was sitting and was waiting to catch a plane home, back to the States. I couldn't help but to think of his loved ones receiving his last letter home and reading the words, "By the time you get this, it'll be just one more day before I see you." And I can imagine them with great anticipation, waiting for the doorbell to ring. However, when the doorbell rings, instead of Sam, it is another man in uniform, bringing the devastating news of Sam's death. Explaining the circumstances surrounding his death, and that it happened at Saigon airport, while he was waiting to catch his ride home.

I was in deep thought when the public address system blared to life, louder than normal, and brought me back to the physical world. It is really amazing to me the things that happen in life that are a six billion to one chance of happening, but it does. The PA system just announced that the assassin of Dr. Martin Luther King had just been captured, his name, James Earl Ray. Because of my thoughts of Sam, I had not paid any attention to the airman who sat across from me, now I did. For the first time, both of us looked across at each other and at our name tags, mine was King and I'm black, his was Ray, and he is white, and then we made eye contact. Was he thinking that I am a relative of Dr. King? Was he thinking that I thought that he was a relative of James Earl Ray? Was he thinking that just because his name is Ray, that I would have an instant disliking and distrust? I don't know how long we both sat there in stunned silence, looking at each other, neither of us spoke. If someone had chanced upon the scene, I'm sure they would have thought that we were statutes.

The PA blared again, broke our fixation, and made an announcement about departure. Half way around the world two individuals encounter one another at a chance meeting, and at the same time, they are informed of the significance and the intertwining of their last names. Who can plan that? The announced departure was my flight. I gathered up my duffle bag and with one final glance, I looked at Airman Ray, he looked at me, I turned and walked away.

Philippines

I arrived in Manila and checked in at the Visiting Enlisted Men's Quarters. I was going to be here for three days and four nights, without any assignment. I just had to report to the Physical Training (PT) complex the next day to start my physical exam. I was free to do whatever I wanted. Wow! This was like an unscheduled R&R (Rest & Recuperation). It just so happened that I met two navy guys Joel and Kevin checking in about the same time who were also going through the same physical training. They were being screened for possible candidacy to the Naval Academy.   None of us knew each other but a quick friendship developed. Since we literally had nothing to do, we decided we would rent a car and check out the city of Manila. Manila is the capital city of the Philippine Islands and the traffic was New York stylish. We visited Museums, and other tourist places until dark. Since we had the exam the next day, we didn't want to stay out too late, so we started heading back to base. We turned down this one street and it was wide but eerily empty. It was obviously a thoroughfare so we couldn't figure out why there was no traffic. The street had a mandatory left bend, and as we made the turn, we immediately found out why the street was devoid of traffic. One way. The street was four lanes wide and all four lanes had a string of cars coming our way. I was not driving. Fortunately, the fella that was driving had quick reactions. He immediately put the vehicle in reverse and gunned the engine. The oncoming cars in our lane slowed down. The others did not. It felt a little strange looking at someone in a car next to you going forward and you going backwards. Folks in the cars on both sides thought it was really funny. I have to give it to the driving skills of our driver. He didn't lose it and was able to extricate (military talk) us from the predicament in which we found ourselves. Once on the road to the base, we began to laugh until we grew hoarse. Nothing like danger to bond friendship.

The next morning, we went together to take or physical exam. It just wasn't an inspect the body exam, it was truly a physical exam. We had to run the mile, see how high we could jump, crawl under obstacles, climb over obstacles and many other athletic events. After that, we then went for a physical exam. This exam was unlike any exam that I had ever taken before. They had machines that I had never seen before. And they had more doctors poking, stabbing, and going, "Uuum," than I had ever had before. When it was all said and done, I passed with flying colors and was informed that if I chose to become a pilot, I was flight qualified. The other two passed as well. We started the exam around 7:00 AM and we finished a little after noon. As we were walking to get something to eat, we met these two gorgeous girls that were stewardess on one of the many airlines that fly in to Manila. They looked Filipino but probably had mixed heritage since they were about three inches taller than the average Filipino. We asked them to join us for lunch and they did. As the day wore on, there was discussion about going to the movies. That became a little awkward. Two of them, three of us. We secretly pulled straws to see which one of us would voluntarily "have some things to do back at the barracks." Myself and Kevin pulled the long straws. Joel was a good sport about it. Throughout the day, he was the most quiet anyway and showed the least interest. He waved as he left. Kevin and I spent the rest of the evening in the girl's company.

Corregidor

We had made plans to go to Corregidor the next day, so we got up fairly early to get on the road. Corregidor is known as the Headquarters for General MacArthur and the "remote" palace for the King and Queen of the Philippine Islands. Both of these venues were of WWII. Corregidor was also designated as an island fortress, the first line of defense for the Philippine mainland, and is about six miles off the coast. The w aters between Corregidor and the mainland are considered "deep waters" so ocean going vessels often plow the waters (something we found out later).   So, we set off to find a place where we could rent a boat to take us over to the Island.   We found this little village that had a guide that would take us there…in a dug-out outrigger, with about a 10 HP engine. It normally would seat two plus the

guide. We had three. The engine had a wooden cover or a box over it that the guide said could and often works as a seat for a fourth person. I chose the engine box as my perch. With the ocean current helping us along, it took us about 45 minutes to get there. From a distance, the island looked extremely peaceful and the evidence of the violence that took place on this island was covered up by a lot of greenery. The beach area was fairly unassuming and was not built up as is shown in a recent photo (see **Fig. 20-1**). The island has a natural cove, with reefs to help break up the waves. On the channel side, we were having some good size swells, but not huge. However, once we got past the reefs, the water became real calm and smooth. We just glided up on the sand. We got out and pulled the dugout, outrigger further up on the sand so high tide wouldn't pull it back into the ocean. There was a native on the island that came out of a hut to greet us. The two spoke Tagalog (ta-ga-la) for a few moments then the native approach us to establish a price for his services. We bantered back and forth a little until we both grinned and said, "deal." He had an old WWII jeep that had a diesel engine that he has kept running since the war. Of course, the island was not big enough to put a lot of miles on it; and there were a lot of ways to make fuel for a diesel. Anyhow we set off to tour the Island. I took many a picture of the island (slides really that I have not been able to locate. The photos contained herein were collected from the web). We got in trouble within the first few moments of being on the island. It happened In the Malinta Tunnel, our first stop on the tour, which was about two hundred yards from the cove (see **Fig. 20-2**). This was the main tunnel on the island and had multiple purposes. This tunnel bore right through the mountain to permit access to the other part of the island where a landing strip had been carved out of the foliage. Without the tunnel, it probably would have taken a day's hike to get from one part to the other part of the island.

The tunnel itself was probably the length of two and a half football fields (see **Fig. 20-3**). The following is a description from a website about the Malinta tunnel on Corregidor:

Fig. 20-2

"The tunnel system under Malinta Hill was the most extensive construction on Corregidor. It consisted of a main east-west passage 826 feet (252 m) long with a 24 foot (7.6 m) diameter and had 25 lateral passages, each about 400 feet (120 m) long, branching out at regular intervals from each side of the main passage. A separate system of tunnels north of this main tunnel housed the underground hospital and had its own 12 laterals and space for 1,000 beds. The facility could be reached either through the main tunnel or by a separate outside entrance on the north side of Malinta Hill. The Navy tunnel system, which lay opposite the hospital, under the south side of Malinta was connected to the main tunnel by a partially completed low passageway through the quartermaster storage lateral. East of this was Malinta Tunnel, *location of Gen. Douglas MacArthur's headquarters. Reinforced with concrete walls, floors, and overhead arches, blowers to furnish fresh air, and a double-track electric tramway line along the east-west passage, the Malinta Tunnel furnished bombproof shelter for the hospital, headquarters, and shops, as well as a maze of underground storehouses."* (Example of office area, see **Fig. 20-4**)

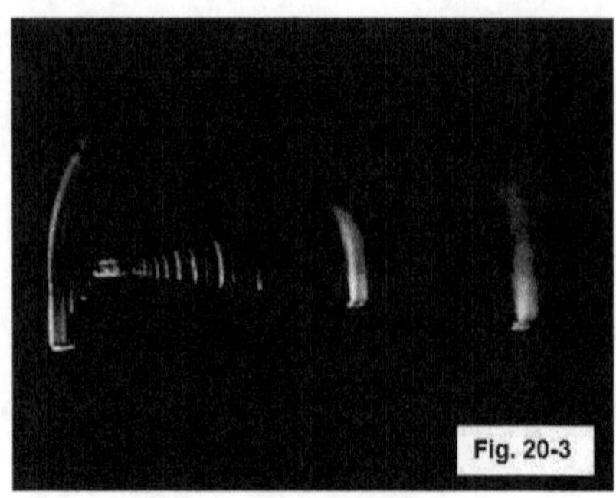

Fig. 20-3

The native driver took us inside of the Malinta tunnel and said that he would wait for us to return. We took the one flashlight and set off to explore the Royal chambers, Gen. MacArthur's headquarters and the 1000 bed hospital. We were amazed at the complexity of the tunnels; that they intertwined with one another, and just represented an amazing engineering feat. We were deep in one of the side tunnels when, wouldn't you know it Murphy decided to call, the "Law of Murphy" that is. This law states that "If something can go wrong, it will," but I add "and, it will pick the most inconvenient time to go wrong." The one flashlight between us decided to stop operating. It didn't go dim over time, it just stopped operating. We were in black as I have never seen black before. There was no ambient light coming in anywhere. We followed each other's voices to come together and discussed what we should do.

Trying to fix the flashlight in that darkness was out of the question. If we dropped a part, there was no way that we would have been able to find it. We had to get to a place where we could see. We had no choice but to grope in the dark for one of the walls, pick a direction and follow our hands as we moved them along the wall. We had to cross several intersections where, believe it or not, geometry came into use. Three points determine a straight line. Well, one of us would walk away, take about 10 to 15 steps from the two of us. The next person would follow his voice, tag and then continue walking for another 10 - 15 steps. As best as the second person could, he would try to keep the other two voices in close alignment. By doing so, we essentially established three points, and formed a fairly straight line. This prevented us from walking in circles and made sure we were continuing along the same path as the wall in which we were leaving. It felt like eternity. I had not read the Bible much at that time so At the time I didn't know that a verse in scripture makes reference to the "outer darkness." However, as I think back on that time, "darkness" is a euphemism; I know I would not want to spend eternity in that blackness.

Fig 20-4 Office Complex

How long we progressed in this blackness I don't recall. We walked and walked, tripping and stumbling over many obstacles, but trying to keep to the wall as much as possible. There was no time in which all of us got away from a wall, even at the intersections. One person was always in touch. At one point, someone said, "Hey, can you see your hand?" Remarkably, we could, barely. Light was coming in somewhere. Now that we knew that there really was "Light at the end of the tunnel," our spirits lifted. We followed this light source until we came out of one of the small entrances on the side of the mountain, just big enough for one person at a time to enter. Why this entrance was here was a little puzzling. This entrance didn't lead to anything and the trail which lead to it was overgrown by foliage. Our thought was that it was an emergency escape or entryway. It was as though it was carved out of the mountain just for us. It was our savior.

We were so immersed in what we were seeing that we forgot about fixing the flashlight. We were awe struck at the visible evidence of the violence that happened here so long ago. The entrance we were in was "L" shaped. I'm sure this was done so that enemy soldiers could not shoot directly into the tunnel, but the bullets would hit the flat wall opposite the opening. As we looked at the wall facing the opening, we were amazed at the many pock marks in the wall. There was not a flat surface bigger than a quarter anywhere on the wall. I closed my eyes, ran my fingers across the wall, and immediately the cacophony of sounds, hundreds of rifles being shot, hand grenades going off, artillery rounds exploding, men screaming, the ground shaking, rocks cracking and becoming like deadly missiles, all seemed so real. I was lost to another world. Time had no relevance. Not sure what broke the trance, but all of us came back to our world at about the same time. We remembered the flashlight. We took the flashlight apart and put it back together again. We were never sure why it malfunctioned, except that it was meant for us to find this little obscure entry way. We probably never would have found it if the flashlight had not malfunctioned. Once again, we entered the carved-out mountain; and once again, trusting in our one flashlight continued our tour through the living quarters and offices. As we exited one of the side tunnels into the main tunnel, we ended up being about a hundred yards from where our guide was waiting for us in his jeep. He gave a shout and came for us in what appeared to be a very hurried manner. We knew he was going to be very angry with us for taking so long. He no sooner stopped the jeep when he asked us,

"Where did you come from, what tunnel did you come out of?"

We showed him. He turned pale and almost fainted.

As it turned out, we were only about 15 yards from the end of the tunnel, heading toward the airfield. "Come with me." The guide said.

We walked to the end of the tunnel and then about another 15 yards along the base of the mountain. He pointed to a pile of old artillery shells, bombs, hand grenades and other explosive that we couldn't identify. The guide said, "As MacArthur's army withdrew, they would set booby traps whenever they vacated parts of the island or fortification. This being the headquarters and royal palace, this part of the tunnel had more booby traps than other parts of the island. We have been cleaning out these tunnels for booby traps for years. We get a demolition team in here every once in a while, and they go through the tunnels looking for trip wires along the ground or tied to furniture. Whenever they find something, they will disarm the bombs or explosives; then, we just stack them here. The tunnel that you just came out of has never been cleaned of booby traps! Didn't you see the signs?" Of course, we didn't. We didn't have a

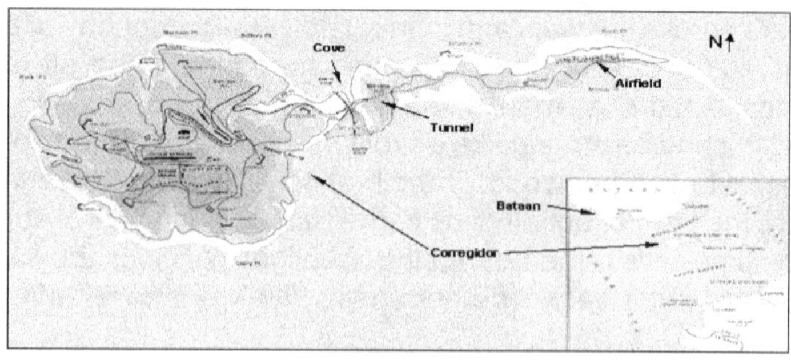

flashlight that worked. The innocence of youth. Yea! We just looked at each other and grinned. We had looked death in the eye and survived. Before we would get back to the mainland, death would once again have an opportunity to look upon us.

Fig. 20-6

In a somber mood, I think more so for the guide than ourselves, we walked back to the jeep. From there we went to visit the airfield. There was not much standing and the runway itself was pretty much overgrown by the jungle, so we didn't stay very long. We turned around and headed back toward the tunnel. Once we went through the tunnel and to the other side of the island, it really got interesting. Corregidor is strategically placed (see **Fig. 20-5**) and its fortification controlled the entrance to Manila Bay and the Philippine capital, Manila. Some of the islands biggest guns were positioned to protect the bay and had very limited movement from side to side (see **Fig. 20-6**) although a smaller version had more maneuverability (**Fig 20-7**). The planners of Corregidor thought that any attempt to conquer the Philippines would target Manila, and as a result would have to come through Manila Bay. The big guns of Corregidor were ready. However, during the battle for Corregidor, these guns had very little impact. They were facing away from the mainland. The Japanese conquered the mainland first and set up fortifications themselves on the Bataan peninsula, the closest land mass to Corregidor. Bataan itself was the sight

of several bloody battles, one in which John Wayne was killed (in the movies that is). Everywhere we went, there were bullet holes, and craters from mortars, bombs and shells from navy ships (see **Fig. 20-8,9,10,11, & 12**). It is hard to imagine the destruction and think of the fierceness of the fighting that went on for days.

Fig. 20-10

Fig. 20-7

Fig. 20-8

Fig. 20-9

Fig. 20-11

The defenders of Corregidor were taking heavy losses, but they were giving as much as they were taking. One mortar placement, consisting of about four mortars, was exacting a heavy toll on the Japanese navy. These units themselves were just so effective that they had the capacity to turn the capricious tide of war into the favor of the island defenders (see **Fig. 20 13 & 14**).

A gun crew on a Japanese navy ship, contained inside a gun turret, were in a routine, reach over, grab the lever that would place a high explosive (HE) round into the gun barrel, grab another lever that would shove the round into place, grab a silk bag of gunpowder, toss it into the breach, grab a second bag, toss it into the breach, grab another lever to close the breach…fire. They did this over and over.   Even though many wore ear

Fig. 20-12

protectors, the tremendous noise and the sustained rate of fire would cause many of them to lose their hearing. One of these crews, performing the loading sequence, over and over, were not aware that they were loading the one shell that would determine the outcome of the battle for Corregidor.   This one shell, after being loaded in the breach, the silk bags of gunpowder placed behind it, the breach closed, was waiting in darkness, waiting for its destiny. The command to fire was given, the shell followed the "rifling" in the barrel and began its spinning rotation that would cause it to fly straight and true. As it left the barrel, it joined a formation of shells aimed at the island, but none of the other shells would have such a profound effect.

Gaining altitude, it arched over other smaller navy vessels, and traversed the open waters of the sea. The whole island of Corregidor could be seen from its highest altitude, the flashes of small and automatic gunfire, the larger flashes of hand grenades

Fig. 20-14

and the even larger flashes from the flight of navy shells indiscriminately impacting vehicles, buildings and the defenders themselves. It wasn't until the shell passed through its apogee or highest point and angled downward that its fate with destiny was known. On the island, members of the mortar crew knew that they were having a devastating effect on the Japanese navy ships and was doing all they could to increase their rate of fire. One of the things they did to speed up the process was to move the mortar rounds from underground storage and stack them next to each of the four mortars. It was highly dangerous, but the pre-stacking decreased the amount of time it took to position the rounds and fire the mortars.   The shell

Fig. 20-13

from the Japanese ship began to descend until it crossed over the cove, the cratered beach, passed the smoking Malinta Tunnel, and the ground up vegetation. In an eerie premonition, one of the defenders felt the angel of death, looked up and for a heartbeat, saw the one shell destined to turn the tide of this battle. The defender didn't have time to be scared. The shell, like a bean bag toss, came through the firing hole of the steel reinforced concrete bunker of the huge mortars, and exploded. The explosion ignited the stored mortar rounds. The resulting explosion was so powerful that it shook the whole island, it literally threw one of the mortars 100 yards away, and fighting on the island came to a complete standstill.

If this was compared to a football game the following would be equivalent. You're playing a superior team whom you have held in check for almost two quarters. You have the football and driving for a potential score. A passing play is called, the ball is caught and the receiver is about to cross the goal line. At the end of the play, a defensive player doesn't go for the tackle, he goes for the ball, a fumble. The defense picks up the ball and starts running back the other way, toward their end zone. The quarterback, gets hurt trying to tackle the runner, gets taken out of the play with a resultant concussion and won't return for the game, the opposing team scores and the clock runs out for the first half of play. You can imagine the swing in emotions. Playing against a superior team, about to score, only to be scored upon. Not only that, but the key to your offense, your starting quarterback gets taken out of the game. Imagine the mood of the two teams as they enter the locker room. One jubilant, the other very somber.

Regardless of where an island defender was or whom he was fighting, when the mortars blew up, he knew it marked the beginning of their demise. The change in the mood of the fighters was palpable. One jubilant, the other very somber. The battle for Corregidor truly became defensive after the loss of the mortars, and the island itself was lost shortly thereafter.

Each place we visited on the island had its own story and the evidence of the bravery, the sacrifice, and the willingness to fight and die for freedom. As I pondered over the imagined carnage, of which time itself could not erase all of the evidence, I thought, what would make a person give their life to a cause, and by their very act, would eliminate them from experiencing any benefit from that cause. Up to now, my experience in Thailand, in support of the Vietnam War, had not provided me with an answer. However, my later experiences in Thailand did, and can be summed up in one word…"Honor."   We soon completed the rounds and our tour guide said it was getting late and we needed to head back to the beach. I think the three of us were a different person leaving than when we arrived. We were seeing, first hand, the effects of a military campaign. We were candidates for a military academy. What lesson could we learn, what value do we put on human life, knowing that one day in the future we may give a command that will cost the lives of many. It was good for us to see the inglorious side of war.

Back to the Mainland

In a somber mood but richer in experience we retraced our trail and arrived at the cove. We gave the tour guide a good-sized tip and thanked him for his knowledge and history of the island. The time was now evening and we had about two hours before dark. The tour guide lent us a hand as we carried our dugout to the waters. We shook hands around one more time, we jumped in the boat (**Fig. 21-1**) Slightly different from the picture, our canoe had a 10 hp engine stuffed in it), and the tour guide gave us a push off. None of us, including the boat guide, were prepared for what we would be facing on our return trip.

The shape of Corregidor and the reef at the cove entrance provides a natural harbor and protection from the waves of the ocean. In our 10 HP dugout canoe, we crossed over the protective

Fig. 21-1

reef and entered the channel. The channel was a little choppy but not bad. We continued toward the mainland. After about a half hour it was obvious our progress was nowhere near what we experienced on the way out. We were going against the current and the ocean swells were gaining in size. Soon thereafter, two things happened: 1) We got out the paddles since the engine was not producing enough power to move us forward; and, 2) We started taking on water. Joel and Kevin began paddling and I, with a half-gallon sized container, began bailing water over the side. Since I was perched on top of the engine; and sitting higher in the boat, I was feeling the full effect of the rolling ocean. I felt like a rodeo rider. Because of the up and down and sideways movement of the boat, I had to hold on with one hand while I was bailing with the other. In one of my rhythmic up and down motions, reaching in to the boat, scraping water off the bottom, sitting up and dumping the water over the side, I saw something that was breathtaking. In the distance I saw a freighter perfectly centered and blocking out the setting sun. It was gorgeous. The sun could not be seen but rays looked like they were emanating from the ship itself. (See **Fig. 21-2**) Marvelous. We all stared at this incredible sight for as long as we dared, then we got back to our survival. Yes, it slowly began to sink in (no pun intended) that we had entered into a fight with nature. On my perch or "look-out" station, I could easily see Corregidor and the mainland. Oc casionally I would look before and aft and proclaim, "If we go down, Corregidor is closer." It was a long time before I would look up and say, "If we go down, the mainland is closer." There were no life jackets, and the only thing that could be used for floatation devices would be one gallon gas cans that were now being consumed by the engine at a questionable rate. The fight was fully engaged. Kevin and Joel rowed harder and I bailed water faster.

Remember that freighter. The one that looked so fantastic as it blocked out the sun. Well, it wasn't looking so good now. As I rose up, in one of my cycles to dump my filled half-gallon size container of water, I saw that same freighter, now heading directly toward us. The sun was extremely low on the horizon and consequently there was very little light. Maybe it was futile, but we knew we had to get the attention of someone on that ship. If we didn't, we wouldn't stand a chance. We were on a collision course.

Joel and Kevin stopped paddling and s upported me as I stood up in the dugout and waved a white T-shirt. We didn't know if we could be heard, but all four of us were screaming at the top of our lungs.   The ship got closer.   The ship was now close enough that we were able to recognize individuals on the fore-deck (see **Fig 21-3**). We kept screaming, I kept waving. I'm sure we were praying somewhere in there as well; we had to have been. Suddenly one of two people on the bow of the ship saw us, pointed, and ran (we presume to a phone) to communicate to the bridge. Almost immediately we could see the bow wave of one side of the ship increase while the other side diminished. Was it going to be enough? *Let me put this in perspective; it takes about a half mile radius for a Navy destroyer to reverse course and about three miles for a carrier. This was a freighter, turning or stopping quickly was not a high priority in its engineering.* There was a flurry of activity on the side of the ship facing us as it seemed like all the crew members came and lined the railing. Unlike most "looky-loo's" who, on the highways, slowdown to see the after-effects of an accident, this crew was waiting to see one in the making.

Slowly, oh so slowly we began to see more of one side of the ship. It was turning. It was going to be close. It made it, no, we made it. It turned away enough to miss us. But, we were not out of danger yet. The crew from the ship, as they looked down at us, were yelling and clapping their hands.   They obviously were glad for us as well. By 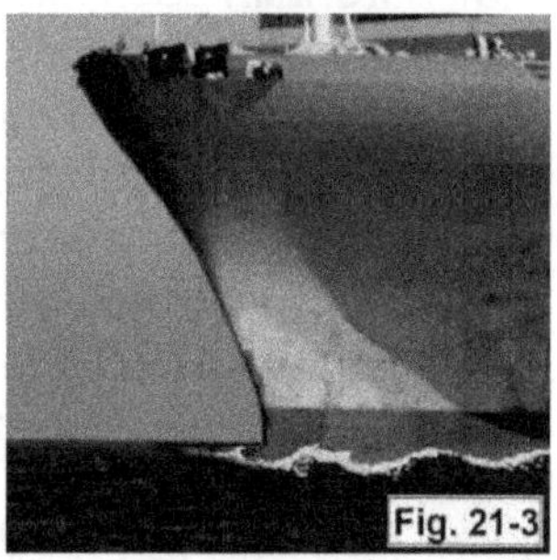 the time the freighter became parallel to us, we were about 50 yards away. The freighter seemed so close I felt like I could reach out and touch it. Slowly it passed us by, not even being impacted by the wind tossed sea. The crew members, clenching their hands above their heads and waving, waved us good bye. Now we had to face the second danger, the wake, associated with this beautiful freighter, that so intermeshed with the sun, that gave us such a glorious sunset.

The sea swells were already increasing, we were still fairly close to being in the middle of the channel, and if we went down, we had a long way to swim to get to the mainland. The wake came upon us with a vengeance. The battle was on. If we are to survive, we had to stop heading for the mainland and turn our little dugout canoe into the surge and take it head on. My pace in bailing water doubled. The paddling increased to give us momentum to get over the crest, if we don't go over, then we go through the wave and take on water. More water than I could ever remove quickly enough with my little half gallon container. There were a couple of times we held our collective breaths as we came out of a trough and approach a crest. We made it, and made another one. And then there was this one wave that was bigger than the others. In fact, in our eyes it looked like a tsunami. Kevin and Joel found extra strength and paddled just a little bit faster. At first it looked like the bow of the canoe was going to penetrate the wave. Not good. With a suddenness that surprised us all, the bow popped up and began to ride the wave. The respite was short lived as we had to immediately focus on the next wave. Slowly, oh so slowly, the wake generated swells began to diminish. After about five minutes of this feverish pace, we felt we could turn and once again head for the mainland. The challenge now was endurance. After that adrenalin rush, we had to once again adopt a rhythm that would carry us to shore. We were tired, but none of us could stop. Without it being spoken, we all knew that each of our lives were in the hands of one another.

After about two- and one-half hours on the water (compared to about 45 minutes outbound), we could begin to have hope of reaching the shore. We were still about a mile out from shore and I was wondering how in the world are we going to find that little patch of land where the village is? As we got a little closer and a little further up the shore, we saw a welcoming sight. A bonfire. The village came out in mass and provided a beacon. As we got closer, we saw people lined up on the shoreline waiting for us to come in. Maybe I shouldn't say "We" since all of the village folks were waiting for our boat guide. However, their waiting highlighted to us the danger that we just encountered. They couldn't see us but many of the villagers were waving torches and flashlights, signaling; and I'm sure, it was their way of expressing hope. The villagers had turned out as a result of their concern for one of their own. Once they spotted us there was shouting, jumping, and the waving became more frantic. As we pulled in to shore, we jumped over the side to drag the canoe onto the sand. It wouldn't budge. The canoe was so waterlogged and riding so low in the water that we couldn't even get close to beaching it. Almost immediately, about six villagers came rushing into the water to help us pull the canoe up on the beach. I think our canoe guide liked the attention he was getting. Already they were asking him what happened, when did we leave Corregidor, was he frightened, etc.? In the canoe, he was rather an unimposing figure, but on the shore and in front of his own people, he transformed into something formidable. He captured that audience so quickly and with such command that Shakespeare would have been proud. The transformation was amazing to watch. The three of us quietly gathered our belongings and left the beach area and headed to the car. We were fairly animated ourselves, discussing the day, our three close encounters with death, the tunnels, the freighter, and the sea, as we made the long drive back to base. We headed back to our respective assignments the following day.

Bangkok

Before returning to Udorn, I had a stop-over in Bangkok I stayed at a hotel in downtown Bangkok, directly across the street from the city park. I arrived late the night before and I was scheduled to spend one more night in Bangkok before I was to be picked up by a cargo plane, another C-130, the following day. I was up fairly early and went walking around downtown for a couple of hours. Upon my return to the hotel, I saw a very attractive Thai, smartly dressed, that looked like she was gathering her things from a counter top. She didn't look like she was in a hurry to go anywhere.   I assumed she worked at the hotel. I went up to her and said "Hello." I was expecting her to snub me, she did. She didn't even turn in my direction. I then greeted her, Sawaa dee kop, koon sa-bye-dee-loo, and asked her where she was from, all in Thai. She stopped doing whatever it was that she had found a sudden interest in, turned around to look at me and said, "You speak with an accent. You must be from up north." At that I started laughing. She didn't say that I had an American accent, she said I had a Northern accent, a Northern

Thai accent. I never thought that I could have an accent from another country; one that would be regional. However, she could tell from my speech that I was from Northern Thailand. She looked very perplexed at my laughter; however, once I explained why I was laughing, she too began to laugh. I told her I was staying at the hotel and was heading back to Udorn in the morning. Since it was close to lunch, I asked if she had time for lunch and a walk in the park immediately thereafter. "I have time for lunch, but I can't do that. Girls that are with G.I.s are automatically assumed to be bad girls, and I am not a bad girl." "Then how about just lunch, we will never leave the hotel; and, therefore you'll never be seen as being a 'Bad Girl.' After all, you're expected to interact with guest at the hotel, and I am a guest." "I too am a guest and I don't have to interact with other guest." "Oh" was I all I could say. Then she laughed. She said the look on my face was worth lunch and a little bad publicity.

Sometime during lunch, she decided that I wasn't the ogre that is often portrayed of us GIs, and agreed to go walking through the park. The day just happened to be "Kite Day," and there were kites all over the place. I took out my camera and just took a picture. Unfortunately, I only took one picture. As it so happened, when I had the film developed, there was not a kite in the photograph. Not on the ground, in the air or in someone's hand. The odds of that happening were enormous, especially if you saw the number of kites floating around. It was a good day to walk in the park. All the various kites made it an interesting walk. We stopped at a little sidewalk café to grab a snack and just sat and watched people go by. As we sat outside on a park bench, we didn't get a lot of attention as I suspected my Thai escort thought we would. It made her more relaxed. We sat there for hours with her segueing into teaching me more Thai and her laughing at my mispronunciations. The afternoon was waning so we decided to walk through the park once more and then head back to the hotel. Once we arrived back at the hotel, imagine my surprise when she asked me what I was doing this evening and would I be willing to accompany her to an event. "Oh no, I can't do that, GIs with Thai girls are considered bad and I'm not a bad GI," was my response. She looked at me in disbelief until she realized that I had mimicked her earlier comment.   She laughed, and said I was a number noong (or number one) GI. It was a good day in Bangkok. Later that evening, just before we left to go to her "event," she surprised me again. She gave me a picture of herself, words on the back, and signed on the front. Unfortunately, the words on the back were in Thai, so I never knew what she wrote; and, she was too embarrassed to translate them. We left to go to her event.

The next morning, I once again boarded a C-130 and headed back to Udorn.

Back on the Flightline

One day on one of my routine maintenance runs, I was working on an F-106 (see **Fig. 23-1**), a base defense air-to-air combat fighter. It is a supersonic, delta wing aircraft that carries four anti-aircraft missiles within its airframe. Four of them are parked near the end of the runway, on an extended ramp, and are always ready to go (see **Fig: 15 – 1**). I was on the top of one of these aircrafts, hanging on to the tail section when I heard a muffled bang. In a war zone, any unusual noise always gets your immediate attention. This got mine. From that day to this, I never recalled how I managed to get off the top of that plane and about 100 yards away, behind a Con-air building, in what were mere seconds. As short as that time was, it was not fast enough. What I saw, and knew, was a mixture of events that could have, should have resulted in a huge explosion. Let me borrow a statement that I had made earlier. "Multiple times during the day, F-4 Fighter jets (see **Fig. 15-2**) would taxi to the arming station prior to take-off. The planes are loaded with bombs and missiles on the flight line, with pins in place, and then the pilot would taxi the plane over to the arming station. Missiles and bombs that are loaded on a plane have a "safety pin" in place to prevent accidental detonation. These pins have about an 18 X 2-inch red tag hanging on them for visibility.

At the arming station, there would be several airmen that would go to each plane and pull the safety pins and arm each weapon just prior to take off. On this particular day, four F-4 Phantoms were at the arming station, jet engines running, having their safety pins removed."

Fig. 23-1

It was about 105 degrees, high humidity and maybe 115 - 120

degrees on the tarmac. As I was working on the F-106, and I heard the "thud" I turned around to determine the source of the noise. What I saw were four F-4s, fully laden with bombs, missiles, and each with two huge 250-gallon fuel tanks. One of the F-4s had dropped both 250-gallon fuel tanks unto the tarmac. The tanks had cracked open and were spilling fuel out on the hot tarmac and in the presence of hot engine exhaust from eight jet engines. One spark and there would be one huge explosion. Remember when I made mention about the "Pucker Factor?" I'm sure at that moment the pilots and their Weapons Control Officers in those jets had a high pucker factor. The base fire trucks, ambulance, bomb squad and other rescue members were on the scene very quickly. Members from the foam trucks started laying down foam about 50 yards away and walked their way in toward the idling jets. Airmen from all over came out to see what would have been a spectacular fireworks display…and as usual, the knoll, by the barracks, had its usual number of looky-loos. As for me, when it is up close and personal, I could do without the fireworks. The rescue squad was good and it didn't take long before they had the situation under control. A disaster was averted that day. The official report was that the tanks were ejected from their stanchions due to a buildup of static electricity. I had doubts about this "official" report since the day had high humidity, not conducive for static electricity build up. It wasn't until 30 years later in a chance meeting of an ex-Air Force office who also was there that day, that I heard what, I believe, is the real truth.

Augmentee & Other Duties

Word had gotten out to several commanders t hat I was a young, energetic, and a smart kid that didn't have problems obeying rules. As a result, I was often asked to perform extra-curricular activities. On one such assignment I was asked if I had any tattoos or any other artificial markings.

Photos taken in helicopter over Laos

"No." Was my response.

"Great. While on this assignment you can never carry any form of identification."

Sometime during my indoctrination, I asked,

"If something happens to me, I won't be in one of those car accidents downtown, will I?"

They just looked at me smiled, and said,

"Yea, he is a fairly bright kid, isn't he?"

I was in a helicopter later that same day, flying east.

Although I didn't know it at the time, my last assignment in Thailand was going to be with Base Defense as an Augmentee. I was going on my seventh month 'in country" and was asked to help guard the base perimeter and other strategic areas of the base such as general supplies, ammunition and fuel. I spent a half day in training,

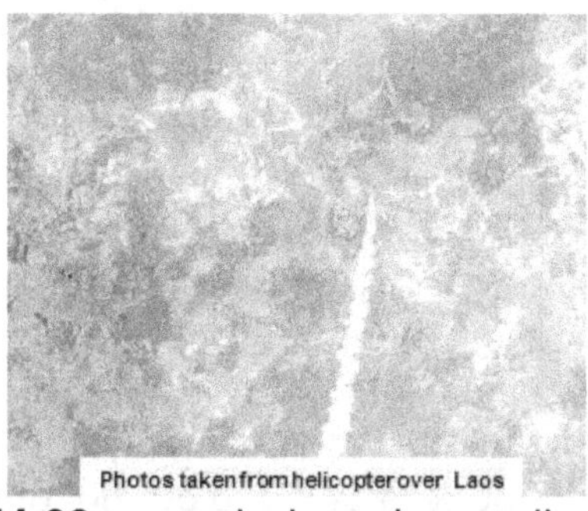
Photos taken from helicopter over Laos

familiarizing myself with the m-16, M-60 grenade launcher, call signs, signals and how to stop an intruder, via walking or vehicle. It didn't take long before the commander discovered that if he wanted to show how well the augmentees were blending in and supporting his regular troops, he would send these individuals to my position. On one such occasion, the following occurred.

The night was dark, maybe a quarter-moon in the sky, and very few clouds. There was hardly a breeze and the night just seemed very still. I was guarding a remote section of the base where it could be easily penetrated by insurgents, with little awareness of their presence. On these kinds of night, it was difficult to not think of home, half a world away. Who's cooking what, who's going to what parties, what would it be like to be in school now, and on and on. Suddenly I heard a faint noise that grew louder by the second. By the sound, I could tell it was some kind of vehicle, not a large one. I couldn't see it yet; it was still obscured by a couple of buildings and a shallow gully. I positioned myself just off the road and got deeper into the shadows. The lights of the vehicle danced off the buildings and the many different containers that were also being stored in the area. Soon I was able to discern that it was a jeep with two occupants inside. It was a typical four-seater of WWII vintage with an open top.

I let them approach, and as soon as they were slightly beyond my position I yelled "Halt! Who goes there?" The driver immediately applied the brakes and came to a stop. I commanded both occupants to not move a muscle until I gave the command. I then commanded the driver to keep his hand on the steering wheel and the passenger to slowly raise his hands above his head.

I told the driver "Right hand first, slowly move your right hand from the steering wheel and place it on top of the windshield. Now slowly do the same thing with your left hand."

I went back to the passenger. "With your hands still above your head move your left hand and slowly place it on the windshield. Now do the same with your right hand."

Instead of complying, the passenger raised up in his seat as if he was going to get out of the vehicle.

"Freeze!"

At the same time, I loaded a round in the chamber. Two things happened. One, he did freeze. Two, he became so pale that he was challenging the moon as to which was brighter.

Even though the engine of the jeep was running, the sound of a bullet being loaded in a chamber is deafening; and, I'm sure to him it sounded like a freight train. With both of his hands now raised he sat down immediately and slowly began putting his right hand on top of the windshield. I originally commanded that he did his left hand first but I can see that he was already visibly shaken so I chose to overlook this minor detail. Once they both had their hands on top of the windshield,

I commanded them to "exit the vehicle from the driver's side."

The passenger started to exit out of his side.

"Freeze." "I will not repeat myself a second time. Listen to every word and comply immediately. Now slide your hands across the top of the windshield. As you exit the vehicle, slowly place one hand behind your head and take 10 steps forward, staying in the headlights."

As they both were standing with their backs toward me, hands on their heads, I noticed that they both were carrying their wallets in their right hip pockets.

"With your left hand, keeping your right hand on your head, reach back and remove your wallet and hold it above your head. Now slowly with your right hand, extract your I.D. and toss it behind you, out of the head lights."

I went to pick up the I.D.s. The Sarge I knew, but when on duty we were told to challenge any and all. I went to pick up the other I.D. Now it was my turn to be nervous... it was a General. Believe me, I thought about leaving them in that position to give me a head start, but there was no place to go. So, I took a deep breath, and gave them the command to be "at ease." To my surprise the General didn't say anything to me.

He looked at the Sarge and said, "Let's get outa here and back to base."

As the Sarge was getting into the Jeep, he looked at me, gave me a hidden thumbs up and winked.

I thought about that exchange the rest of my shift. Wondering what was going to happen when I got back to base. It is amazing how fast rumors and gossip can fly. When the troop truck came with my relief, the word was already out that I had hassled a General and, using a GI vernacular, "my A_ _ was grass."   I figured I would get shipped stateside within the week. We pulled in to base ops and, purposely, I was the last to get out of the vehicle. I was not in a hurry. Usually, Sarge was the one to debrief us, that is to find out if there were any significant events that happened or something that base defense should be made aware of, like a broken fence, evidence of forbidden traffic and such. We were standing at ease when the Sarge came out of the office. But, to our surprise, so did the captain.

The Sarge yelled, "Atteennnd Hut."

We all snapped to.

The captain walked up and down the line.

"I heard this evening that one of you could not tell the difference between enlisted personnel and an officer, and more importantly... a General. How about that?" The captain said.

The captain went on for several minutes about the purpose and value of Augmentees and how essential they are for this base in particular, with me feeling lower and lower. All I wanted then was a hole to crawl into. Oftentimes the service will single out an individual to emphasize a point, but have the whole unit pay the consequences. . .   I thought of the hassle I was going to get from the members of my squad. Oh boy.

Then I heard him say, "Thanks to Airman King,"

Then he paused,

"The General gave us high marks on how you guys have been trained, protect the base, and support our regular guard. Well done gentlemen. Dismissed."

I was stunned. The Sarge pulled me aside to tell me what happened. The General dropped in unannounced to see if in fact Augmentees were a contributing entity and a viable adjunct to the regular Air Patrol or AP. The General requested to visit a couple of places where we were pulling guard duty to find out himself how well trained, we were. He only visited the one, mine. He was so shaken by that experience, especially when I chambered a round, that he was satisfied with the one check. Sarge told me that he purposely drove to my position to show the general how remote some of the guard points are.   The Sarge said that he and the captain had been hearing good reports about me so, he and the captain were confident that I would be "On guard."   Sarge also said that he may put in a request to my division commander to extend my services for another 30 days.

After the episode with the General, things quickly settled into a routine.   I was being assigned to what were called "High Value" targets such as the ammunition dump, the fuel depot and the mechanical storage area. All of these had value in their use, but even more so if we were denied their use.

Fig. 24 -1

Thailand has some real good thunderstorms. Loud, long and boisterous. On one such night, I was assigned to guard the ammo dump. I felt the wind pick up and saw the lightning in the clouds move cl oser and closer. When it came, the leading edge hit with a vengeance. I had on a poncho, but the wind was whipping it all over the place. I decided that I would get out of the rain and wind but still be in position to watch my designated zone for any activity. I moved a couple of boxes to block the wind and hunkered down for the duration, except for my occasional walk arounds. The lightning intensified, illuminating the night as if it was day. On one of these illuminations, I noticed the bed that the ammo was sitting on… "Pierced Steel Planking." For a hundred yards square, there was a bed of long steel planks with holes in it sitting on top of the ground with the ammo sitting on top of the steel and with me sitting on top of the ammo (See **Fig.24 -1**). Talk about a lightning rod. All it would take is one stray lightning bolt and, well, let's just say my tour of duty would be over. It was a strange sensation, almost surreal. I didn't want to sit there, but I didn't want to leave my post either. I could not walk far enough away and be safe, and still be considered as guarding my post. This again is one of those times when I thought, "What is it with responsibility, honor and commitment that would cause someone to do the most irrational thing, sitting on a box of high explosives that in turn are sitting on steel, in a lightning storm?"

During the storm I did have time to think on some things, like the letter I got from a buddy of mine that a friend of ours was killed in 'Nam. I thought about his family, their reaction when they got the bad news. How the hopes and dreams for someone you love can evaporate in a second.   I remember seeing him around campus, all of us so young, and Vietnam was such a far-away place. He was an excellent baseball player and rumor has it that he had received an invitation to tryout at one of the major league camps. But not now. I hope they have baseball in heaven.

I thought about my own family, how dad had been missing for so many years until my sister Victoria, or Vic as I call her, and I found him in Gary Indiana. Years before, my dad had been attacked and struck with a bumper jack. He was attempting to break up a fight that erupted at one of the dances my brothers and their friends were giving. It happened that members from a rival school showed up and the ensuing fight seemed inevitable from the very beginning. During the fight my Dad had a .38 revolver that he pulled out and, sacrificing the ceiling and roof, pulled the trigger. Nothing happened. He pulled the trigger again, nothing happened. His initial actions did cause a lull in the fighting as he did get their attention. But when the firearm didn't fire, he got more than just their attention, one group actually attacked him. He went down in a flurry of activity. Later we found out that my brother had removed the bullets from the chamber and didn't put them back.

A few years later, my father, a cabinet maker, was driving to do a kitchen in Hollywood. Dad was often called JB, and had a great reputation in LA, Hollywood, and Beverly Hills of high-quality work. I remember visiting many mansions in Pacific Palisades, Beverly Hills and the likes.   Anyhow, one day as dad was driving to Hollywood he kept on driving and didn't stop until he got to San Francisco. He was in Frisco for several days before he met a contractor that he was able to convince that he knew cabinetry. He could neither remember his name nor where he was from, but he knew that he could work wood.   The contractor was working for a doctor and asked "JB" to come with him to the doctor's house. There the contractor directed dad to go in the kitchen and tell him what he thought he could do with it. The contractor and the owner followed him around to see if he knew what he was talking about.

It didn't take long before the owner exclaimed, "I want this man to do the job."

The owner of the house took a liking to dad and realized that he was suffering from amnesia. It just so happened that the owner of the house also had "connections."

He told dad. "I have a doctor friend in Canada, just across the border from Detroit, and I believe that he may be able to help you. However, if I help you, you have to help me. I have a car that I need to have driven to Detroit. You drive the car and we'll get you another station wagon to replace the one you have. You can put all your tools in the car and take them with you. We, uh, I'll even provide you up front money to set up shop in Detroit or another city in the area. What do you think?"

Dad finished working on the kitchen, got the car, with suitcases, made room for his tools, got traveling money, and headed east. When he arrived in Detroit, he called the number given him and he then was given an address and directions to get there. At the address given him, he met a couple of guys that treated him extremely well, said he had been accepted as part of the family. After the two guys transferred the suitcases and secured them, they helped dad transfer his tools to a waiting station wagon. Not a new one, but newer than what he had. One of the guys told dad to follow him and that he would take him across the border to a doctor that was expecting him. Dad followed and was lead through the city of Detroit, continuing east and into Canada. The doctor didn't live far from the border, as is the case with most Canadians. Eighty percent of all Canadians live within 200 miles of their Southern border.

Something fell. Senses full alert, adrenaline flooding the system, heart beat accelerating, hearing becoming acute, lying prone on the wet steel planking, water soaking through the various openings within the poncho, head rotating back and forth in an attempt to isolate any accompanying sound. Other than the patter of the rain, no other sound could be heard. I stand up slowly, knowing that now I must make an investigation. I go in the direction where I thought I heard the sound originate. Oh boy. Right at the edge of the ammo storage area is an old shack that has a wooden fence around it. I passed by it several times earlier. The sound came from there. In my mind I thought, "How many bad guys can hide in that thing or even just on the other side of the fence." I check the M-16 once again and have it at the ready. I stoop down, making sure I stay below the height of the fence and move as quietly as I could toward the gate, about five yards away. I am alongside the fence, all is quiet, except for the patter of the rain. As I approach the gate, it was slightly cracked. Not a good sign. I got close enough to the gate to open it with the barrel of the rifle. But before I did, I wrapped the sling to the M-16 around my forearm to make sure no one would be able to snatch it away from me. As I began to poke the barrel through the small opening of the gate, three things, no four things happened all at once; 1) There was lighting and one big bang of thunder; 2) There was a burst of wind; and, 3) The gate opened and banged against itself, …and a stray dog ran out of the gate. The fourth, I almost died. Since it was raining and I was already drenched, I didn't know if I had to change my underwear or not. It all happened so quickly. I thought, "Wow, things like this only happens in the movies." About now, my little perch, sitting on top of high explosives was a welcome thought. Still wary, I checked the other side of the fence and made sure the shack was still boarded tight. It was. I circled the ammo, dump once more, senses still on alert, and made my way back to the self-made perch. Aah, home.

I drifted back into my reverie and my dad. The Canadian doctor took X-rays and did several other studies of my dad's head. His prognosis was a brain tumor, originating from the spot where he had suffered a head trauma, resulting from the blow of the bumper jack. The doctor told my dad that it was inoperable and that he had about 3 – 4 years to live. With the money that his "friends" fronted him, dad moved to Gary Indiana and set up shop as "Ace Cabinets." One day, my oldest brother Bruce, who lived in Indianapolis Indiana, was working in his own cabinet shop, when a friend of his says, "Hey Bruce, I saw your dad working up in Gary the other day. I asked him about you and he didn't remember who you were. I thought I was mistaken, but I know your family, and I know it was him." Bruce contacted my mother and oldest sister, Delores, out in Los Angeles and told them that dad had been spotted. My sister Vic and I coordinated a trip to my brother's home in Indy, with plans to drive up to Gary from there. I was in high school and since the family could not afford it I had to use my own earnings to buy a plane ticket. When we got to Gary, we started asking around if anyone knew of a fella that went by Ace or JB. The second day in the city, we met someone that vaguely remembered someone of that name and told of a place where he "hung out." It took most of the second day to track all the leads that we got, but by 5:00 PM we had found our dad. Even as I write this, it is painful to think of the years lost without my father. It would take several months for my dad to accept that he had a family and longer still before he would come home. By the time my dad made it back to L.A., I was in the service. In fact, I had to get his permission to join since I was 17 at the time.

The next day my Commander called me in his office and said that he has orders for me that will cut my tour of duty in Thailand short. Evidently, I did well on my physical in the Philippines and as a result, I got orders to go to the Air Force Academy Prep School. I had about 10 days left on my Augmentee assignment, but about a week before I left the country. The Commander told me that the Captain of the Air Police had requested that I spend another tour with them, but was informed of my new assignment. He then asked that I finish out my current duties with them before I left. Life is full of choices. My commander gave me the choice to continue with the Augmentee duties or return to my unit. Guard duty gave me four more hours of free time, time that I could spend saying good bye to my friends in the town of Udorn and around the base. I chose to stay with the AP and perform guard duty. That choice was very impacting. Additionally, my reassignment to the Prep School caused a very significant thing to happen or not happen that I would not find out until weeks later. However, once again, it made me realize that guardian angels were working overtime.

The evening of my discussion with my Commander, I was pulling guard duty at one of the parts storage supply depots. It was known as a frequent target by the Pathos Loa (Laotians sympathetic to North Vietnam) due to the type of supplies stored. Each shift of guard duty is about four and a half hours long. The half hour is due to the average time it takes to change out the guards. At the beginning of the shift, there is a lot of things to do to keep and maintain attention and alertness. Walking the perimeter of the area of responsibility, checking for a place to set up a defensive position and just exploring, all are very active things that keeps a person alert. As the shift wears on, boredom, inattention, and fatigue can creep in. The most challenging time in performing guard duty is the last hour of the shift. Moreover, boredom and inattention can happen faster if it is a location that has been guarded previously. This was a location that I had guarded previously, it was late at night, and it was my last hour of duty. Two shots rang out, I hit the dirt, round in chamber, senses full alert, adrenaline flooding the system, heart beat accelerating, hearing becoming acute. I reach for the radio to call for backup. Radio not working. Just before being relieved of duty, we were told to remove the battery from the radio so the next guard can insert a fully charged battery. Additionally, this process speeds up the exchange. We were for anything that can speed the guard exchange process and let us get back to the barracks faster. I reached into my pocket to get the battery, removed the backing of the radio and jammed the battery into the radio. Nothing. Mind you, I'm trying to do this while still keeping my eyes scanning the area, trying to locate my attacker.

The problem is the shape of the battery. The battery looks like a squared off hockey puck, about half the size. The contact is on one of eight possible edges. I think you now understand my plight. I would have had to put the battery in, test the radio, if it didn't work, remove the battery, rotate it, put the battery in, test the radio for a total of four times. If it didn't work after those four times, I would have had to turn it over and repeat the process, all while trying to locate someone that is shooting at you. I gave up on the radio and changed positions. For about five minutes we played cat and mouse. Then I heard a welcoming sound, the cavalry; also known as the Strategic Alert Team (SAT). The cavalry came in the form of two armored jeeps, with three airmen per jeep. It has a mounted .50 caliber machine gun and each airman carries an "over/ under," an M-16 rifle with an M-60 grenade launcher hung underneath. One of the jeeps was driven by the Sargent of the Guards. At the sound of the SAT team and their vehicle, I heard one last sound of skirmishing and then it was quiet. I stayed at the ready. I will say this, I did not challenge Sarge and the SAT team as they can near my post. They were a welcomed sight. I joined up with the SAT team and we did a perimeter check to make sure the area was clear. Who ever was there had gone. I asked Sarge, "How did you know I was in trouble?" He responded, "Airman Blake at the next guard post heard the gunfire, thought you had been shot and asked for immediate backup. He thought that they were coming in his direction next. We didn't know what to expect. We were all relieved to see you alive." For the balance of my guard duty, I never again pulled the battery from my radio prior to being picked up. No one complained.

Departure from Thailand

I saw my Commander again just before I left and he congratulated me on my being selected to go the Academy Prep School. He talked about what an honor it was that he had me to serve under his command. He captured the many things I had done in such a short period of time.

The Commander commented, "Section leader, airman of the month, later chosen to represent the base for airman of the year, the 'didn't happen assignment,' work with the Supply & Warehouse division and their request to extend your assignment, the Augmentee duty where once again a request for your extension was made, and lastly, you got your third stripe in close to record time. All of this in just seven months. We have airmen here a full year that don't get half that much notoriety. God's speed airman and I'll see you once again before you leave."

With that I was dismissed. When I got to the barracks, there was a party going on. It was in full swing as the empty beer cans could attest as they had started being stacked on top of one another.

I asked, "What is the occasion for the party."

"You are. It's your going away party." They said. There  must have been 40 to 50 guys sitting around playing multiple games of Pinochle and Bid Wisk. It wasn't too obvious that I was just an excuse. When I came in, someone immediately put a beer can in my hand, knowing that I didn't drink, much less beer. What I didn't know was that there was a conspiracy to get me drunk before I left the next day. This was quickly discovered as I eventually finished the can that was given me when another immediately materialized. I sat down to play a hand of Pinochle, thinking this would distract my beer benefactors. It didn't. I lost a couple of games, got up walked around, sat my beer can down, oops, where did it go? It took me a while, but eventually I learned that if I walked around with a can, no one tried to give me another. It took about 6 -7 half empty accidentally, on purpose, misplaced cans to figure this out. We were playing rise and fly; that is, if you lost your hand, you rose and flew from the table. At one of my settings at the card table, my partner and I came within one card of running a "Boston." It was my hand, my bid, but boy was my partner disappointed when he discovered that I had misplayed a card. Not that I did anything wrong, it just wasn't the best card to play. He was an avid Pinochle player, had never come that close to a "Boston" or capturing every hand that was played; and, knew how rare the event was.

Others came to my defense, "After all, it is his party and he probably had a few cans that jumbled his brains."

We all laughed. The following day I said my good-byes.

As I was writing this, I started thinking, all this stuff happened and I was only in Thailand for seven months. Wow!

Prep School - Studies

When I arrived at the Academy Prep School, on the Academy grounds in Colorado Springs, Colorado, I was met with about 25 other airmen that were in the Air Force. We were arriving two weeks prior to the rest of the group which were coming in straight from high school. In total, the school would number about 225. It was here at the Prep School where I encountered the harsh reality of prejudice and how to live with it. I also got a lesson in humbleness. Let's talk about the second first.   Recall when I mentioned that, "I continued to be a Sports Writer, had joined the Knights, was on Boys Court, President of Co-op Cabinet, member of Student Body Cabinet and made the Honor Roll?" Well, I thought I was pretty good with the studies and all. After all, I had taken a math class every semester in high school and each of the three times in summer school, to include the summer prior to my 10th grade semester. I knew math, or so I thought. During the 12-month period at the Prep School, I had Algebra I, II, III, IV, Geometry I & II, Trigonometry I & II, and Calculus I & II, and probably something else I don't remember. We also had multiple levels of English, World Geography, Poetry, Literature, Speech and Political Science. We did more in that one year than I did in three years in high school. It was a torrid pace. We were up before dawn, did our Physical Training (PT), ate breakfast and began classes by 7:30 AM. We had 45 minutes for lunch and finished our studies at 4:00 PM. From there we went to intra-mural or inter-school sports. Practice lasted until 6:00PM, dinner at 6:30PM, studied until lights out at 11:00 PM. This repeated itself every day except for Saturday and Sunday. On Saturday, we had practices immediately after lunch until 4:00 PM, and Sunday was a free day for us right after church service.

I was at the Prep School for about two weeks when I received a letter from one of my augmentee buddies back in Thailand. If you recall, the paragraph where I captured my parting conversation with the company Commander in Thailand, I concluded that paragraph by saying, "… my reassignment to the Prep School caused a very significant thing to happen or not happen that I would not find out until weeks later. However, once again, it made me realize that guardian angels were working overtime." As I read the letter my buddy sent me, a chill went up my spine and back again.   The content of the letter went something like this,

"King, you are one hellava lucky guy. The day you left; the base was infiltrated by about six Patho-Loa. (These were guerillas friendly to the cause of North Vietnam). The point of infiltration was your assigned position that night. They penetrated the base and managed to place satchel charges (explosives) against two planes blew them up and escaped. The guy that was at your position never fired a shot, didn't challenge them and didn't even make a call on the radio. We all talked about how different that would have been had you been on post that night. Even the sergeant talked about how aggressive you were and that it was a shame that King wasn't here. Who knows what would have happened.' Take care, we miss you buddy."

As the Sarge alluded to in the letter, I took my assignments seriously. Would I have challenged the infiltrators, I believed I would have. Would they have begun shooting; I believe that they would have. Would I have returned fire, I believe I would have. Was there a possibility that I could have been shot, I believe there would have. I also believe the Lord's timing is right on time. The Lord knew, to the day, when it was time for me to leave Thailand. Otherwise, there is that distinct possibility that I would not be alive today to write this Odyssey. I also think back to the First Sergeant who submitted my name to the Academy, which started the process of my being at the Prep School and ultimately the Air Force Academy. Timing and the Lord's blessing truly has its place.

I spent many of my Saturdays and Sundays staying in the dorm continuing my studies. In comparison to most of the cadets in attendance, I had a lot of catching up to do. The reason for the Prep School existence was to provide training, either in studies or physical conditioning for those individuals who are slated to enter the Air Force Academy the following year. Any cadet graduating from the Prep School, and entering the Academy, has a huge advantage over a candidate who has not. As tough as it was, we knew what the rewards were and as a result, very few dropped out of Prep School. I slowly regained my confidence, but initially I was angry. I was angry at the school system in Los Angeles, which had me thinking that I was trained and prepared, and angry at the Prep School for slapping me in the face with my inadequacies. In Literature, we had an assignment to write something about the time in which we lived and how it may relate to a previous time in America's history. Since this was in the summer of '68, I wrote this eloquent and thought-provoking paper about how the 60's of today was similar to the 60's in President Abraham Lincoln's time. I made mention that the effects of slavery are still present, that we are still experiencing racial divide, and that the country could in fact still have a fighting civil war.

I posed a question, "President Abraham Lincoln, if you were alive today, 100 years later, would you be proud of the America you helped save?"

I said eloquent and thought provoking because I let my room-mate read it and he said, "Wow, you got to let some of the other guys read this."

The paper got passed around before I had a chance to turn it in as my completed assignment. All who read it said they had not given thought on the subject in the way that I had presented it and it really made them think.

As I was writing the paper, I thought about a friend of mine who was killed during the Watts riot of '63. Sure, he was in a place that he shouldn't have been, didn't need to be. His family was very middle class and I never knew him lacking for anything. In fact, his parents had just bought a car and said that it was his after one year of good grades. We all were looking forward to that event. He was shot by the police as he was running from an electronics store with a television in his arms. Did he need the TV? No. He was just young, being foolish, and being caught up in the moment. Still, should he have been shot? Is a TV more valuable than human life? Evidently at the time, and in Watts, there was no question. So when I began to think of comparing the 1960's to the 1860's, I didn't see much progress. Years later, in February 2010, I read an article that confirmed some of my comments that I had written in the paper.

Nashville TN - Fifth Avenue downtown bustles with activity on a blustery recent afternoon. People of all races mingle: This could be any midsize city in the United States, circa 2010.

Fifty years ago, [or 1960] things were different. The stores along Fifth Avenue — specifically, their lunch counters — and the city itself were the site of a battle that also played out in dozens of other cities in the South. The fight pitted black college students and a few of their white peers against the city's white power structure and its downtown merchants over the right to sit down and eat lunch. At the time, blacks could spend money in those stores but couldn't eat at the stores' lunch counters. The lunch counter of 1960 was the equivalent of fast-food restaurants today. Hamburger chains were just beginning to appear on the American landscape. Ray Kroc had opened his first McDonald's about five years earlier; Burger King had gone national just the year before. People wanting a sandwich or a hamburger popped over to the lunch counter of department stores, drugstores and five-and-dime stores to have a bite…except black people.
By Larry Copeland, USA TODAY

When I got my paper back from the instructor, I was dumbfounded by what I saw. He bled (red ink) on it so much that he must have gone through two ink pens. I was dejected at the apparent rejection. There was not one word of praise or encouragement. I was so upset and angry that I just threw the paper away. To this day I wish that I had kept it. The sentence structure, grammar, and syntax may not have been right; however, the content had high value as evidenced by those who read it. I had learned humility in a very harsh manner. A thought that occurred to me much later was the possibility of my hitting a nerve of the instructor. Maybe what I was saying was so right-on that it was challenging his beliefs and how he wanted to perceive society. I will never know. However, one thing I was certain of, from that day forward, I was determined to improve in all my studies. I was not going to experience that level of rejection again.

Prep School - Football

Growing up in LA, a group of us in the neighborhood would go over to the park where the Los Angeles Coliseum and Museums are located. On the grounds there were many expanses of wide-open areas that were ideal for playing football. During the summer break from school, we would often meet kids from other neighborhoods and play, neighborhood against neighborhood. Oddly enough, the games would get heated, but nary a fight ever broke out. I was a small child growing up, but when it came to football, I was fearless and played beyond my size. Never was there a time that I was chosen last. It was amazing that we did not have the need for an ambulance every week. I don't recall that one was ever called. We didn't play touch football, this was full blown tackle football, without helmets or pads. This was my environment.

Now I'm at the Prep School, trying out for the school football team. All 25 or so of us that arrived at the school early went to tryout for the team. It was grueling; and, purposely so. It was a weeding process. By the time the other cadets arrived, the first bunch of tryouts were cut in half. Moreover, those of us who made it through the first weeding were not given any consideration. We were thrown in with the rest who were trying out for the team for the first time. When this second weeding process was completed only myself and a cadet named Clemente survived of the original 25. Of course, there were many who dropped out that were trying out from the second group. A lot of the guys who made the team were actually "recruited" by the Academy and were sent to the Prep School to shore up a few little deficiencies. Clemente and myself were not looked upon fondly. It was like, "Didn't these guys get the hint?" I was six feet and only 160 lbs, but I knew I could play football. The head coach was an Air Force Captain from Alabama. Very quickly it became apparent that he had his favorites. I was not one of them.

Coach had selected his "A" team and relegated me to the "D" team as far as running backs were concerned. We had just played our first game over the weekend and were making adjustments to the defense. We won the game, but the Coach felt the defense could be tightened up a little bit. To do this, the Coach had the "A" team defense against the "B" team offense and the offense was going nowhere. It looked like the defense was tightening up really good. I was standing on the sideline.

One of the other coaches who was very supportive, called out "King."

I ran up to him "Yes, Coach."

"Go in and show them how it's done." He then pulled me close and said, "I know you can do it, show the rest."

With those words of encouragement, I ran to the huddle and, even as the running back, I took control. The first play, five yards. Cheers went up from the sideline. The head coach turned to look at the players on the sideline, but said nothing. After all, it was just one play and probably a fluke. The "A" team defense was on the field.   Next play, another five yards. Then ten yards. The offense was getting charged up and it was obviously having a negative effect on the defense.

The Coach yelled to the defense from the sideline, "Better hold them this down or there will be hell to pay."

The defense held us that down. The next down however, I broke free for what would have been a touchdown had we been on a playing field. The Coach was furious. He stopped the scrimmage and began chastising the defense with words I would not write in this paper. The other coaches however came over to us and congratulated us on our playing.

The one coach in particular said, "Great job King."

Our next game was a night game with the number two rated junior college team in the state. It was a tough battle. By this time, I had moved up one notch to the number three running back position. I didn't see action the whole game. Surprisingly, to a lot of folks in the stands, we were winning, but only by four points. We knew we were good and this game would verify what we all believed. Anyhow, up by four points, two minutes left in the game, and Coach calls his next favorite player to go in and carry the ball. It didn't matter that I had consistently out played both running backs, Coach couldn't get over his dislike for me. So, I think to further exasperate me, and to get me to quit the team, he sends in the other running back. I'm standing on the sideline. What happened next gave me such an emotional roller coaster ride I didn't know to laugh or cry.   The second favorite son takes the hand-off, gets hit, and fumbles the ball. The other team picks up the ball runs about 60 yards and is caught around the eight-yard line. Three plays later they score. Game is over. We lose by three points.

The following week, I'm moved to the number two slot and second favorite son quits the team. We were 10 – 2 for the season. I got to play more often, but Coach made sure I *got no* recognition. In one game we played, I was racking up some yardage. However, every time we got close to scoring, Coach would either send in a pass play or call the fullback's number. We scored more than thirty points that game and I totaled more than 100 yards, but no score. As we were getting on the bus, Coach looked at me and then over me. He didn't say a word.

But the other coaches, everyone said, "Good game King."

On the ride back to the Prep School, the one coach, left his seat, came back to me and said, "That was a really good game."

He then went and sat back down. I never could fully understand why Coach didn't like me nor appreciated my value to the team. I was neither a goof off nor a lazy person, and neither was I the only Black cadet on the team. Still, it was painful to know that, someone of significant influence in your life didn't like you for no apparent reason, or for a reason that is all too apparent.

Prep School - Lacrosse

Fig.

After the football season I tried out for Lacrosse. I didn't even know what the game was but I heard that you get to hit people, and with that I was interested. The game itself is like playing hockey on a football field. The "puck" is a ball about the size of a regular sized orange and the "stick" is of various sizes with webbing at one end. Players are festooned with a helmet, with cage, and pads on the shoulder and arms (see **Fig. 28 – 1**). The goalie, since he often has to block a fairly hard ball, traveling at speeds up to 110 mph, has the addition of pads on his hips, thighs, and protection for future generations. Many of us that joined the team had never played before. I tried out and made the team in the middie position. A typical Lacrosse team would have three forwards (attackers), three middies (transition players), three defensemen (defense), and a goalie. We had three forwards, four middies and two defense players who had played before. I got in a few times our first three games but not much.

It is not easy trying to catch an orange in a triangular shape webbing, at the end of a four-foot stick, while running, while an opposing player is bumping you, and the orange is traveling about 80 mph. We all were getting better, but I don't think we won any of our first three games. Our fourth game, we were down 3 – 0 at the half. The other team had these small but fast little guys in which our big 200-pound defensive guys couldn't keep up. Within the first minute of the second half, they scored again. Besides being painful, I was tired of sitting on the bench.

I went up to the coach and said, "Coach, our defensive guys can't keep up with them little guys, put me in as defense."

At first it seemed like the coach started to say, "Go sit down until I call you," which is standard for most coaches when a player tries to get into a game on his own volition. But then abruptly, there was a little sparkle in his eyes as he thought of the possibilities. No worse than what we are playing now, and what if it does work?

"King, take middle D" the coach said.

As is often said, "Be careful what you ask for, you may get it."

I wanted to get into the game, and I wanted to play defense, but I didn't want to play middle D. The problem with middle D is, when the goalie is out of his box, the middle D goes into the box and covers the

goal. The goalie has full head to toe protection. As a middie, I only had head, shoulders, and arms protection. Now there is a reason why the goalie has full protection. The velocity and mass of that orange ball creates welts when it hits and also for a few errant sticks that may contact the goalie in the foray to defend the goal. Talk about being put in harm's way. But I'm a soldier. "It's not for me to ask for reason or why, but to do or die." I went forth to do battle. With this change in strategy, we were able to shut down their offense. They didn't score another point, and the swing energized our offense. We lost the game but we scored a couple of points and I started at middle D every game thereafter. There were a many of times after the games that I enumerated my abrasions as a result of frequent contact with a projectile traveling at high rate of speed.

While at the Prep School, I met Sergeant Best, who worked in the cafeteria. He and his wife would invite me over occasionally for a Sunday Dinner. We really developed a close friendship and his home was like a home away from home. Sometimes he would invite me to go to a party in Denver with him and his wife. On one of those trips, I met a young lady name Delores. I was never one to develop fast relationships and I certainly would not, could not while at the Prep School or the Academy.   Still, it was good just to have someone of the opposite sex to talk to. We maintained loose contact during the rest of my time at the Prep School.

Fig. 28-4

Fig. 28-3

The editor of the Prep School yearbook heard that I was a sports reporter for my high school newspaper and, because of that, recruited me to do some writing for our yearbook.   He later discovered that I had a little drawing talent and then asked me to do some drawings that would be dividers for the different sections of the year book. Shown on this page and following are excerpts of some of those drawings. **Fig 28-2** is a drawing of the Prep School Commander, rendition of Oedipus, of Shakespeare fame with books in the background symbolizing literary studies. The building is what our dorms looked like. **Fig 28 – 3** represent the two mascots of the two schools; the husky of the Prep School and the Falcon for the Air Force Academy. The symbol in the background with dates represent the year in which we would graduate from the two schools. This section contained the individual photos of all the Prep School cadets.

Fig 28 – 4 is obviously associated with sports. Candid shots of the various games that we played were in this section. For such a small population, we were very competitive in every sport in which we competed against other schools. Students from the schools

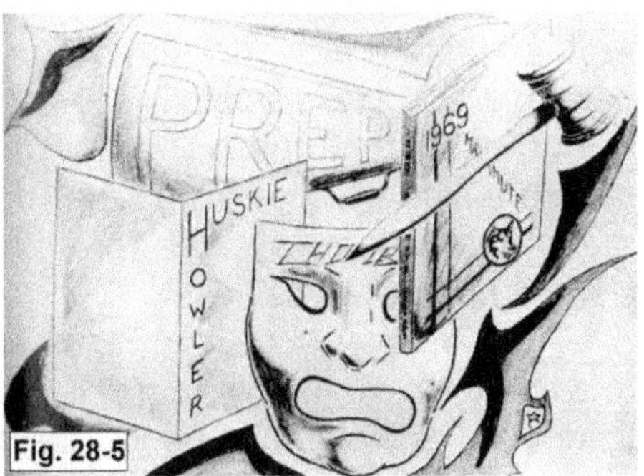

Fig. 28-5

that we played were often surprised when they heard we had less than 400 students. They were even more surprised when we came out as the victor. **Figure 28 – 5** represented the mixture of studies that we undertook at the school. There was math, writing, drama, meetings - rules of conduct, Singing or Chorus (for you that know me, don't laugh), and extracurricular activities.

The book in the drawing is what the front page of the year book looks like. This drawing changed several times as the cover had several iterations it went through before it settled on this format. Since this drawing was going to be in the yearbook, it really required close coordination.   Then there was graduation.

Academy - Becoming a Doolie; First Day

The Air Force Academy is a very striking facility. It is nestled in the slopes at the southern end of the Rocky Mountains range, (see **Fig. 29 – 1**) just a few miles from Pikes Peak, in Colorado Springs, CO. It is the newest of the Military Academies, both in age of its creation and the facility itself. The one structure that dominates the Academy courtyard is the Ultra-modern Chapel (See **Fig. 29 - 2, 3**). There are many different structures on the grounds besides classrooms and dorms; such as a state-of-the-art training facility, where Olympians train, an indoor field-house for soccer, tract and football and an acre size cafeteria where all 1200 cadets can eat at one time. The Fig 29 -1 grounds encompasses about 600 acres, with varying terrain and is about a mile above sea level.

The main campus is essentially a square. The chapel is located on the western side, dorms are on the south and north side, the cafeteria and classrooms are on the eastern side. In the middle of all these structures is a large grassy area, surrounded by what cadets called the Terrazzo (see **Fig. 29 – 4**). The Terrazzo was the general assembly area for all of the cadets. The dorm that I was in, I believe was called "C-2" (arrow).

My first day at the Air Force Academy was unlike any day of most other cadets. During the war, airlines offered half priced tickets to any service personnel that flew in uniform. I took advantage of this discount and flew in what are called "Dress Blues." They are very blah in their styling and after 40 years the Air Force still had not changed them. They don't capture the imagination in any way, at least not for a branch of the service that is new and embraces new technologies. The Marines look far better. Anyhow, I fly in my dress blues, land at the civilian airport in Colorado Springs and go to the baggage pickup area. I wait, and wait, and wait. No luggage. I go to the lost luggage area and give the

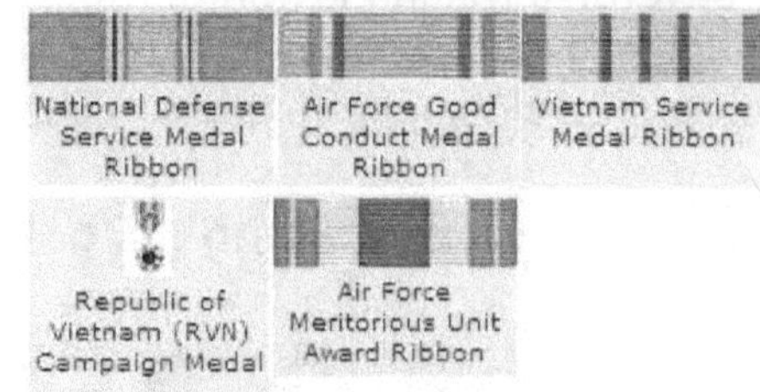

Fig 29 – 2

airlines all the information I knew to give. After filing a claim, I found a telephone booth to call the Air Force Academy to find out how I may be picked up. I called the number given me for pick-up. I was standing at the designated spot when the short bus arrived. The driver stopped, and you can tell he looked puzzled. He opened the door and I proceeded to get on the bus.

He stopped me and said, "This bus is for new cadets for the Air Force Academy."

I responded "I am a new cadet and I am reporting to the Academy."

Then he started laughing.

"Oh boy, you are either going to be loved or hated up there."

Oh how right he was. Most freshmen, for the Academy, come right out of high school and are still wet behind the ears. Me, I had three stripes on my arms, in the Air Force, wearing dress blues, adorned with two rows of ribbons, one a distinguish unit citation, and the one most notable, the Vietnam service ribbon. I was wearing what all of the cadets at the Academy were looking, waiting, and hoping to wear. My intention was to change into civilian clothes once I landed at the airport, since I didn't want to draw unnecessary attention. I kinda thought it wouldn't be good to show up in what I was wearing. The lost luggage changed that idea. The attention I didn't want, I got.

When us newbies, freshmen, or doolies check into the Academy, the senior class is not present. The recently graduated doolies or sophomores and juniors run the show. You can imagine their curiosity when they see a uniformed doolie, everyone else is in civies, walking like a robot, chin tucked, head immobile, eyes forward, etc. Their curiosity was piqued even further when they see a doolie, in uniform with a double row of ribbons. Need to explain something here. A doolie at any of the academies is not permitted to walk natural. They must square all corners, may not walk in the diagonal, unless the sidewalk goes in that direction, must keep eyes forward, and chin tucked in. A doolie caught walking in any other manner was subject to immediate correction, harassment, and possible receipt of demerits. The one basic benefit, walking in this manner, is that it improves peripheral vision, a distinct asset when in combat, either as a soldier on the ground or flying a plane. It also creates the subtle if not an obvious awareness that doolies are not equal to upper classmen.

For breakfast, lunch, and dinner, while in uniform, there was not a time, coming back from the cafeteria, (we went to the cafeteria in formation – returned to our rooms individually) that I was not called out by an upperclassman with the intent to scrutinize me up and down. Many of the uppers would have this makeshift frown on their face in objection to their world being invaded by an enlisted person. The stripes were not on my uniform (I had taken them off), didn't have to be, the uniform spoke for itself. This frown would remain until I got close enough to them and they were able to recognize the Vietnam service ribbon. Upon recognition (and they all knew what that ribbon looked like) their countenance would change to a look of surprise. Because of my service in 'Nam, I was granted to walk at ease and join in on their conversation. Every time though, even if I didn't join their conversation, a new conversation would develop, and it would always be about the war in Vietnam. "What was it like?" "What did you do?" "How long were you there?" "Did you see any action?" etc. It started at breakfast. The group was a little bigger at lunch. By dinner, it was almost a crowd. This continued for the next two days until my luggage arrived. By then the word was out that there was a doolie walking around that saw service in South East Asia (SEA).

That evening I got the members of my squad together and asked them if they had any service or ROTC or Reserve Officer Training Corps time. None of them had. I informed them that I will be willing to teach them about spit shining boots, making beds so quarters bounce, how to keep the room clean and other things to pass room and personal inspection. "I have been doing this for about 18 months now, so I think I know what I am doing. I will be available every night at a certain time. I will not come looking for you, but I will take time with whoever shows up." I had already started sharing a lot of things with my roommate, who was about 5' 5", Irish decent, red hair, and from the state of Washington. He spoke up and said to the group, "I can't believe all the stuff he's shown me already, and we just got here." That was my first day at the Academy.

All of us doolies spent the next two days processing, getting sized for clothing, taking test, getting our rooms together and other administrative activities.

The Third Day

And then there was the third day. The two days prior, we were up and, on the terrazzo, ready to march, at least our attempt at marching, walk to the cafeteria by 7:30 AM. This morning we were up, dressed in our new fatigues, and in formation before the dawn. As usual, we lined up, in formation, facing the dorm. There were about 100 of us in our flight and maybe four flights in our squadron. The upperclassman, a sophomore, that had been herding us the previous two days shouted, "Flight, abooout face." As close to unison that we could muster, we faced the opposite direction. And then, in darkness, we stood there. We stood in the darkness for an indeterminable amount of time. Nothing was said. Then we heard this slow, low rumble. At this point, I believe I have to tell the story from a real doolies' perspective. I'm sure the impact on me, with my prior basic training, prep school and service experience, was much, much less than those right out of high school. Let me step into the shoes of someone that just graduated from high school. The story follows:

> *This morning was different than other mornings. First of all, we were waken way before dawn, told to get dressed in two minutes and fall out (meaning to be at our formation and standing at parade rest). It wasn't difficult to have this premonition that this day was going to be much different than the others. Secondly, it was the first day that we were dressed in our fatigues and looked kinda military. Thirdly, while in formation, we were told to "about face." With that command, there was a slight tremble that began with my knees that slowly worked its way up and down my whole body. Then there was this barely perceptible, thump, thump, thump, that grew louder by the second. That slight tremble began to magnify in unison with each successive thump. That thump reverberated off the walls of the buildings and added to its---------- Then I found my heart began to beat in unison with that thump*

as well. When I thought it could get no louder, suddenly there was this eerie silence. I was anticipating another "thump," but it didn't come. It stopped. Stopping is not good. I don't know how long the silence lasted, it felt like eternity, but I was neither prepared for the noise that erupted nor for its closeness, and I mean closeness. I don't even remember all what was said, but out of the darkness this voice materialized right next to my ear. It didn't matter what was said, all I know is that fear gripped me and held on so tightly that it was difficult for me to breath. I stood there, gasping for breath, with this disembodied spirit yelling and screaming at me, saying something about my not being worth the speck of a fly and that I certainly could not have come from the mold that a man was made from, why the Air Force chose to waste time and money on me is really questionable, etc., etc. This continued for what also felt like eternity. Out of the corner of my eye, I saw some of my classmates' doing push-ups, jumping jacks, squats, and other physical exercises. "Not me Lord, not me" I prayed. Maybe I prayed too late, but no sooner had I finished praying that thought, that this big 250 plus pound upper classman was in my face. His face consumed my whole awareness. My brain would not, could not focus on anything else. If I was commanded to kiss my sister, at that moment I would have done so (what a thought, ugh). My mind just lost all contact with my body. I was doing push-ups. 11...12...13. How did I get down here? How did I get to 11 push-ups when I don't remember the first one? Suddenly, there was quiet once again. It enveloped us like a blanket. My body, however, would not get quiet, it had been taxed, challenged, put on high alert, and it was not ready to go into neutral. It stayed poised for action….Time passed. Well, maybe it's over…Oh, my God! I think many of us had to have a change in pants. There wasn't this yelling and screaming, but this small whisper that once again materialized right beside our ear. I think we all were prepared for a repeat of the yelling and screaming, the quiet whisper

*was just too sudden, so surprising, and unexpected.
Mama.*

I saw many of my classmates scared out of their boots. The Academies rarely have candidates from the "streets" enter. For many of my classmates, this would have been the first time that they felt that they were under attack, felt defenseless and nowhere or no one to turn to. For me, I detached my brain from my body and just put it in "response mode." And for that I almost got more attention than I wanted, again. I was thinking about my classmates, what they were going through, how they were feeling and how were the upperclassmen enjoying this "breaking in" session. Evidently, I had a slight smile on my face that I didn't know that I had. An upperclassman who snuck up and got in my face, noticed my grin, and oh boy, did he jump on me. It was a good thing that it was dark. I would have really hated it if he would have been able to tell who I was. I ended up doing push-ups, jumping jacks, and a few other stuff. I wasn't smiling anymore. Eventually, the squadron commander, someone us doolies had not met, and all the other upper classmen came and joined our ranks. We did height alignment. Left to right, front to back, where the shortest person in the flight would be right front, and the tallest would be left, rear. Following the adjustment, we were given the command to march to breakfast. My classmates never marched better in their life.

When we got to the cafeteria, we were introduced to a rigid eating program. Everything we ate had to be small enough that after three chews, we could swallow it and recite any of the learning material that had been given us. Of course, the upperclassmen or uppies loved to wait until we had just put food in our mouth to ask us a question. The routine was like this. We marched in and stood behind the chair at our assigned table. The cafeteria was a full acre under one roof, unobstructed. We could not talk to anyone. If we got lost, and couldn't find our table, we didn't eat. We stood behind our chair until given the command to sit. We sat down, hands on our laps, eyes straight ahead. Until we were given the command to "proceed," we didn't know what we were eating, except by smell, since we couldn't look down at the food. Once given the command, whatever was on the plate that required cutting, was cut, one piece at a time in a small portion.

The knife was set in its place, the fork used to bring the tiny morsel to our mouth. Making sure all angles were squared and that no triangles were used. On the return, the path of the fork is re-traced and the fork is then placed on the table in its former position. When the fork is on the table, only then, could us doolies begin to chew our food. And then, of course would come the questions. There was no benefit to having the right answer to any question asked, that was expected. There were, however, negatives if a question was not answered correctly or the response was too long in coming. After every response to a question, an uppie, there may be four at an oblong table of 12, would either say good or proceed. If they don't say either, then that doolie would have to sit at the table, hands in his lap, staring straight ahead, until something is said. Occasionally an uppie would forget to give the release command and that one doolie would be sitting at attention while the rest of us would be eating, and…we could not remind the uppie that he forgot. It was remarkable that we ever got enough to eat to sustain us for the day. Sometimes we didn't. We were always in hunger. The food tasted great, a lot of variety, but for us doolies, we just didn't get much of it. On Sundays, it was a little bit more relaxed and we got to eat more. Sundays began to have a special meaning in more ways than one. We were nourished in body and spirit.

The Cafeteria

Whenever we did something that got notoriety, that is recognition by all the cadets in the cafeteria, we were rewarded by being able to eat our meal "at ease." It didn't take long for our squad to figure that out. We often would do something to gain attention, sing (at least the others did), help serve uppies at another table, or just about anything. A significant event for us though was an infiltration event at 2:00 AM in the morning. The seniors, that are also the cadet commanders, don't eat on the ground floor with the rest of the 1150 cadets. There are about 50 seniors that sit on a balcony that has a stairway with locking door in the rear of the balcony. Our assignment, which we placed upon ourselves, was to gain access to the balcony and decorate it with our homemade signs, and leave our call sign that included our flight and squad number. Six of us woke early one morning, gathered the needed material we had stashed away and took a week to collect, and began our quest. We had been at the Academy a couple of months by now and had improved in our ability to move fast while maintaining low observability. We dodged a few uppies (why they were up at this time of morning we didn't know) as we made it out of the dorm. Next, we had to make it across the two-hundred-yard terrazzo, which is flat open space, access the cafeteria (by which way I won't divulge), and then get to the balcony area. Since the back entrance was locked, we made a human ladder for one of us to scale, acquire access to the balcony, and unlock the back door for the rest of us to enter. Upon successful ingress, we began our decorating. Everything had to be neat, nothing permanent and there could be no damage to any item, after all, we would be telling the whole cadet world we had performed this brazen escapade. We made table cloths out of butcher paper, decorated it with drawings and classic statements and reset the table for that morning's breakfast. To finish off, we hung a banner on the front of the balcony.

We had taken a huge risk. If our efforts were not accepted by the senior command team, there is no telling what our punishment would be. In order to not jeopardize our whole flight and squad, only the six of us knew what we had planned. So, if any of our classmates were asked, they could honestly plead ignorance. But if it was accepted, we all stood to gain. All we could do now was to make if back to our rooms, undiscovered, and wait. That morning's wakeup call came early and with a lot of apprehension. Since I have been at the Academy, I had never received a gig slip. (Every doolie carries a piece of paper that any uppie can request and write us up if we are caught doing something wrong.) It's not that I never did anything wrong, I just never got caught. But in this, there would be no hiding from what is in store for me and the other five that participated in the late-night excursion. Fli-i-i-ght, Attention. *Oh boy, here we go.* R-i-i-ght Face. *I think I'm going to be dog meat.* Forwa-a-a-rd Harch. *What were we thinking these past six days?* Thump… thump…thump, the boots of 125 cadets began to hit the terrazzo, in unison. My heart began to get in rhythm and beat in unison with each step, pounding so loud that I was sure the cadet next to me could hear it. Fli-i-i-ght, Halt. We began to file into the cafeteria.

Today, the cafeteria seemed like a huge whale, ready to swallow me whole. I and the other five doolies went in, stood at attention at our table. We couldn't help but to notice that there was a buzz in the air as there were more conversations being had than normal.

Occasionally we heard, "Look at that."
As one, all the cadets stood, said the pledge of allegiance and sat down. The six of us sat ramrod straight, (I think my hair even straighten a little). It got very quiet as (we heard later) the command team on the balcony was still standing.

Then we heard over the public address system, "cadets of flight 39, squad 04, Atte-e-e-ntion! The six of us shot to our feet. We stood at attention. All 3000 pair of eyes were on us. Thump…Thump… Thump. Heart pounding, I am sure the whole table could hear it beating.

The senior commander began "I recognize that doolies often do things to gain recognition, but this is the most brazen and audacious piece of work that I have seen since I have been eating in the cafeteria."

The commander said a few more lines and finished up with, "it is our responsibility to teach you team work. You succeed as a team and you fail as a team. As I said in my opening statement, what I see before me is brazen and audacious. But nevertheless, I have to honor boldness. Doolies,… at ease!"

It took every ounce of strength to keep my feet and not collapse as there was a rapid cessation of adrenalin that was running through my body. What the commander did was put the whole 1200-member doolie class at ease to eat their meal. We were not free to talk, except to say, "pass the salt," but who cared about talking. Eating at last. Eating at last, thank God Almighty. Eating at last.

The uppies at our table congratulated us on what we had done and asked, "So, what do you plan to do next to top that?"

At the moment, that was for the future to determine, we were just enjoying the food.

A-Team

The Academy has 15 Situation Exercises that test the skills of a unit, assess its ability to work as a team, evaluates aptitude for leadership, and must be completed within 15 minutes. Situations like carrying a wounded soldier (see **Fig. 32 - 1** or crossing a river, or scaling a tall structure (see **Fig. 32 -2**). Here again I will not divulge what these exercises are since I don't know if the Academy is still performing the same drills; and, I still feel honor bound. Our squad's performance during these exercises gave us recognition, unbeknownst to us, as the A-team. These exercises were extremely challenging as the average number of exercises completed by any one team was two, the most was five. For each exercise the leadership was rotated. Here again, my experience in the regular Air Force proved invaluable. As we were given instructions for each exercise, I made sure I was within earshot of the person providing the instructions. In this way, there were two people hearing what needed to be done. As a result; we always had a brief discussion prior to tackling the project to compare what we both heard before agreeing on a strategy. As the day wore on, we began to notice that more and more officers and uppies began to observe our progress through the exercises. Since we didn't have anything to compare to, we didn't know that this gathering attention was a little unusual.

At one exercise we had a distinct choice to make; however, since I was older and had more experience, the team agreed to go with my recommendation, even though I was not the designated leader at the time. That choice by the team made the difference in our success. We found out later that had we made the other choice, we would not have been able to complete the exercise. It just so happened that we completed this exercise in record time. When we got through our tenth exercise, completing five, the gathering audience began to clap. They knew we tied the record for the number of completed exercises, we didn't. In fact, we thought we were doing fairly poorly and they were clapping to

acknowledge that we managed to complete another one. We were running about 50% completion, and that didn't seem very good in my books. We didn't complete the next exercise; however, we did complete the following exercise and the one following that. At the end of the day, the team completed seven exercises, a new record. Broke the existing time on three exercises and established a mark, for one of the three, (the one mentioned above where a choice had to be made) that the Academy believes will never be broken. We completed our day, not aware of the buzz that we caused and the buzz that was circling at the higher levels.

Fig 32 – 2

A couple of weeks later our squad was facing another obstacle/ Exercise course. There were many things we did that counted toward our individual performance, however, whenever we did any physical activity, I always made sure we always pared off. I likened it to a "Wingman," and the members of the squad took to it very readily. This day, our first obstacle was a 4-story frame of a simulated building. We had to scale the outside wall, cross the crisscrossing beamed roof, and descend on the other side. In our squad we had a heavy-weight that I'll call Big John. For this event, I made sure Big John and I were partners. Where ever we went and whatever we did, as usual, there were a couple of uppies that were monitoring and scoring our progress. The uppies looked on as we were given the signal to begin. We ascended the side of the structure, pairs working together. It was like rock climbing, where you had to look for every hand and toe hold. Very few of the beams ran parallel to the ground or to each other. Big John was a challenge, he didn't have the necessary upper body strength to pull himself up when fully stretched. But that was why we were in teams. No one left behind or to themselves.

Surprisingly, Big John and I got to the top just slightly behind the others. The squad was waiting at the top. By now I was the undisputed leader of the squad, and I informed the rest to continue down the other side.   Big John and I made better and faster progress going down than coming up. As Big John touched the ground and I jumped from my position, the cadet monitor, shaking his head, stopped his watch.

He looked at us, still shaking his head, and said, "Now I know why you are called the 'A-team.'"

This was the first time we had heard that expression in reference to us and we asked what did he mean?

He said," Well, when you guys first came to my station, you guys looked like all the other doolies. There didn't seem to be anything special about you. I had heard how well you did at the big exercise and the number of records you set, so I was expecting to see a squad of 12, all 200 pounds, and six feet tall. Instead, I saw a squad no different than any other that I had seen today. I checked my notes just to make sure I was monitoring and timing the right squad. And yep, right squad. But now I am a believer. We don't always state the conditions in which we grade an exercise. This particular exercise is based on a total team time, not individual times. Even though you didn't know and no one told you it was going to be a team effort, you guys did what obviously was natural for your squad. The way you guys paired off, helping each other, talking to one another, making sure you all knew where the other guys were, it was a beautiful thing. As far as I am concerned, you guys have earned your nickname. I have said enough... get on to your next assignment. Oh, by the way, you guys have just produced the fastest time on the course."

One thing about notoriety, once you get it, everybody wants to see for themselves, what is so special? We weren't trying to be special; we were just trying to do the best we could. What I believe made us special was our philosophy and how we chose to operate as a team. We each had a "wingman"; we paired our weak and our strengths together; and, we made a point that we would fail together or succeed together.

Survival Training

I think the Academy has 60,000 acres that butts up against national land that is often used by the Academy for training purposes. One bright sunny morning about 500 of us boarded buses and set off into the wilderness of the Colorado Rockies. It was a fairly long ride because we were traveling up and down the country-side on minimally kept back roads.   Where we were eventually dropped off looked extremely isolated and felt uninhabited. There were plenty of trees, but no sound. The forest just didn't have the feel of life in it. What we found out later was that we were the second group of doolies coming into the area, the first group essentially cause the animals of the area to vacate and seek shelter elsewhere.   Our squad of twelve were given two live rabbits, the equivalent to two canteens of water apiece, four matches, a couple of "K" rations (WW II era, no MREs), salt and iodine tablets, a poncho, tent, and a few other odds and ends. We had to stay out for a week. Additionally, we had to go to class on escape and evasion techniques and how to live off the land. We learned how to trap squirrel, rabbit, and other small game.

Learning how to capture small game was interesting, however, the group before us either caught the small game or chased them away. We still set our traps in the off chance that a squirrel would see our trap, felt pity on us and threw itself into the wire noose. Didn't happen. That was why we were given the two rabbits. We had to kill them dress them, set up a parachute as a smoke hut and smoke the meat. It had to last us for the remainder of the week, and smoking was about the only way we would be able to preserve the meat. Our first night out, the stars were beautiful, the air was comfortable, the moon cast a soft glow and all us guys sat around our campfire talking about how great it would be to be up here with our girlfriends. The second night, it was nice to be here with our girlfriends with a nice cold bottle of beer. The third night, it was a girlfriend, nice cold bottle of beer and some fried chicken. By the time the fourth night came, it was just fried chicken and a bottle of beer. It's amazing how priorities can change.

During the week, we were kept busy learning how to eat off the land, where to get water, how to stay warm and many other things to assure our survival. It wasn't that someone came and got us to take us to the various training venues, we were just given coordinates, map, compass, and a time. It was up to us to find our way. To help supplement our smoked rabbit, we were given one unit of K-rations left over from WWII. It contained cigarettes, a Pemmican bar, a Hershey bar, fruit cocktail, dry soup mix, plus a few other items. Not much. Since I didn't smoke, I would often trade the cigarettes for other food items. Sometimes, if someone who smokes didn't want to negotiate, I would light a cigarette, wave it around a little bit, and just let it burn. It's amazing what a burning cigarette will do to the nose of those who smoke. It wouldn't take long before others, would come running up. After that, a bidding war would start and it wouldn't take long before I got what I wanted and a little more since I had to "waste a cigarette." To this day, however, I will not go close to anything that says, "Pemmican." Once again, our squad excelled. So much so that we found out that our overseer had placed a bet on our performance for a steak dinner. The bet was that our squad would out-perform several other squads on our 50-mile hike. The 50-mile hike was on the evening of, the next to the last day, and the morning of the last day. We were given coordinates to a landmark that we had to identify and have confirmed before we were given coordinates to the next marker. That evening, after 25 miles of crossing gullies, streams, climbing down cliff faces, climbing up cliff faces, and other terrain barriers, we came within 100 yards of the final marker and about an hour ahead of the next squad. The next day was repeated. Another 25 miles and more gullies, streams and cliff faces. That evening we ate steak; and, thought about our girlfriends again. Oh yeah!

The Uppie

When I first arrived at the Academy, and I had to march around in my service uniform with the ribbons and citations, one upper classman took noticed. He didn't necessarily like the special treatment I was receiving; how others of his classmates would permit me to walk with them, at ease, have conversation with them, at ease, etc. I had not paid any special attention to him until one evening I was in my dorm room with my roommate and squadron commander. Our own room is the one place where it is a sanctuary, where we can relax and be at ease, unless an inspection is underway. This Uppie happened to walk by our door while the Squadron Commander (SC) was sitting on my bed, relaxed and having conversation with us two doolies (again to remind you having the SC talking to doolies was rare). The Uppie walked past, stopped, backed up and entered our room. He commanded me to attention, I did. He started asking me to cite the various memory lines we had to know. I did. What happened next surprised me. My SC got up and left the room.

This Uppie was totally out of line, and my SC did not attempt to stop the harassment, but chose to leave me to my fate. My respect for the SC fell a many a notch.

"I've been watching you since the day you came. You think you're better than all the other doolies, just because you got to walk and talk? Must have felt good to be treated like you were an Uppie."

The Uppie was not content with me quoting memory verses since I was hitting them all, he began yelling to have me do jumping jacks, 4-point exercises and running in place. After about five minutes of this tirade, and my turning a bright red, my anger began a slow boil. About this time, my roommate slipped out of the room and disappeared. I figured he didn't want to get involved. Smart guy. The pot was getting hotter. Sweat was pouring off of my body.

"Get your knees higher… Higher…Faster…Faster."

In my mind I'm weighing my options. I'm gonna deck this guy was the most frequent option I was considering when. . . revelation upon revelation. This Uppie wants me to deck him. If I did that, I would go before the cadet commanders and be tried, found guilty of hitting a superior officer, and be recommended for discharge, a dishonorable discharge. There went my G.I. bill, my ticket for schooling. There went my VA assistance, my ticket for buying my first home. Ohh, this guy was very, very malicious. Boy, was I glad that I thought through the consequences, or as I often say, connected the dots. The anger boiling up inside of me dissipated and a smile slowly began to find its way across my face. The change in the Uppie was tangible. We began to swap facades. The anger I had was slowly replaced with a smile, and the smile the Uppie had began to be replaced with anger. I began running in place faster, lifting my legs higher, screaming the memory lines louder, all with a big ole Cheshire grin on my face. Now I was having fun. The Uppie got so mad that I think I started seeing steam coming out of his ears. He turned and stormed out of the room. He no sooner left than my roommate and six other squad members came running in. I am dripping in sweat, exhausted, but elated. I asked them why were they all here. My roommate, when he left the room, went to get members of our squad. They had been waiting right outside the room, heard and saw all of what had just happened. They said they weren't there as curiosity seekers, they were there just in case. They were concerned that I was gonna kill the guy. A dishonorable discharge was one thing, murder was something else. We all began to laugh and began to re-tell the incident. It got funnier at each telling.

It didn't stop there.

One day, returning to my room from the Cadet Store, a small convenience store, I passed the same Uppie that came into my room. He fell in behind me and followed me until we were in a fairly isolated section of the hallway. He knew he was doing wrong and is why he didn't want any witnesses.

"Doolie, I want you to go up on the terrazzo, walk around one of the planes on exhibit five times and quote your memory verse as you walk around."

"Yes Sir." I replied.

I changed direction toward the terrazzo. As soon as I got out of his sight, I changed direction and headed toward my dorm room. On the way, I saw a couple of my classmates and we all began walking together. Wouldn't you know it, I bump into the same Uppie, again.

As we are all walking up the stairs,

"Doolie." He says.

I say nothing.

"There is no way you could have walked around that plane and be here by now."

I still said nothing.

"What's wrong, cats got your tongue?"

I still said nothing.

"Alright, don't talk then."

At that I turned looked him in the eye and said, "Yes Sir."

Steam once again began to emerge from his ears and trailed behind him as he hurried on his way. My classmates followed me to my room and as soon as they crossed the threshold, they burst out laughing. They said they could hardly contain themselves when they heard me say nothing to all the Uppie's comment except when he said,

"Don't talk then,"

and, I said, "Yes Sir,"

An order that I willfully obeyed. Once again, the story got funnier as it was re-told. In total, I probably had 5 - 6 incidences with my Uppie friend.

Memories

I have fond memories of my time at the Academy, my classmates, friendships that were forged under duress, the many challenges that had to be overcome, the instructors that I met, and the many opportunities that were provided me. I remember Big O, a football player and one of my closest friends at the Academy. Another was my roommate who was a redhead and was from the state of Washington. One day I overhead two colonels talking to each other and one was telling the other a peculiar scene he had observed about a week ago. The Academy was playing a basketball game with one of the colleges in the area. At the concession stand, was this very pretty and shapely blonde. Mind you, at the Academy we don't come in contact with ladies very often. My roommate and I just happened to be beside her. What I didn't see and this colonel observed was my roommate checking out this blonde, looking her up and down and really sizing her up. And "up" is the operative word. He is 5' 5" and she, about six feet. I can just imagine that picture.

One of the things that the Academy drove home was the motto. "I will neither lie, cheat, nor steal, nor tolerate amongst us anyone who does." Once I entered the Academy, I had a better appreciation of the "cheating scandal" that were occasionally reported in the newspaper. What was considered "cheating" at the Academy would have been acceptable at most colleges. Still, it was the standard and it was enforced, not by the administration, but by the cadets themselves. Anyone who knew or tolerated an infraction was judged equally as guilty.

There was a Lieutenant Page, who I kept in contact with until very recently, and Colonel Anderson, who is a main character in another story. I think of the painting I did on one of the dorm walls, and wonder if it is still there. It was a painting of an F-4 Phantom taking off of a runway, bomb racks full, climbing vertical, with a rendering of the Udorn airbase as a backdrop. I think I even included "the shack" in the painting as well. I also painted in the F-104's, couldn't forget them as they are a reminder of where I was when the F-4 dropped its external fuel tanks on the cross-way. Many an Uppie came by to state their appreciation for the painting. I think of Sergeant Best, a good friend that I met at the Prep School for the Academy. In fact, his friendship started me on my final chapter with the Academy.

Changes

I met Sergeant Best and his wife while I was at the Academy Prep School. He and his wife would often invite me to Sunday dinner and occasionally let me use their '57 Chevy to go into town. I tried to never take advantage of their hospitality and we grew very close. Once I entered the Academy, a standing order is to "Not fraternize with enlisted personnel." This meant that I should no longer have any association with Sergeant Best and his Wife. No longer go over for Sunday dinner. No longer use their car for occasional runs. Not good. To me, this order felt like discrimination. I didn't like discrimination being on the receiving end, and I certainly didn't want to be on the initiating end.

One day one of my classmates came to me and made a comment that caused me to reflect and assess where I was with relationship to the Academy; and, what impact it was having on my actions, my thoughts, my personality, my life.

My classmate said, "Mel you're really good at calling cadence and everyone likes it when you do call it, but I've noticed a change in the language and the kind of cadences you're calling. It seems like they're getting more risqué. It's not that we don't like them, if it was anybody else, we wouldn't have noticed, and I wouldn't have said anything, but this is not like you."

I mentioned earlier that I became one of the frequent cadence callers in the squad. They started out very innocently but began to degrade over time. I had not noticed the degradation until one of my classmates brought it to my attention.   I'll repeat one of the earlier ones that I used to sing out:

> Stand-up hook-up, shuffle to the door
> I'm gonna jump on the count of four
> If my chute don't open wide
> I gotta nother by side
> If the one on my side don't work
> I'm gonna die when I hit the dirt
> Sound off..One... two, Sound off, three...four
> Sound off, 1...2...3,4

It was the subtle things that seemed to have been creeping into my personality that was changing me. When the change was brought to my attention, I began to assess what was changing. I took several days to contemplate this observance and what it meant to me. In the month of October, 1969, I compiled a letter of resignation from the Academy and submitted it to my squadron commander. I had no idea the furor this action would cause.

The Final Chapter - Resignation

I submitted my resignation just before dinner, by the time dinner was over and I returned back to my dorm, over 20 of my classmates were waiting for me in my room. The underground railroad was alive and well. Remember, us doolies could not talk, unless spoken to, outside of our dorm room. Yet, there were 20 of my classmates in my room who heard about my resignation. This was the beginning of many similar sessions. I even had upper classmen stop by to talk and ask why? One thing that became very apparent to me, the more I had to defend my decision, the more I believed it was the right choice for me.

A couple of days after my resignation, Colonel Anderson called me into his office. He headed up the Office of Administration, and I had an opportunity to have dinner with him and his wife a couple of times. He was a great guy and I admired him a lot. At one time he was the Squadron Commander for the Thunderbirds.

When I came to his office, he asked me the now, very familiar question, "Why?"

I went through my litany of reasons as he sat quietly and listened. As I wound to a close, he made several proposals to entice me to withdraw my resignation. One was a ride with the Thunderbirds during one of their practice sessions. Wow! Tempti-i-i-ng! I held to my guns. He then invited me to dinner with him, his wife, and another colonel that I knew and his wife. This other colonel was the pilot of the T-33 of which I had an introductory ride (See **Fig. 37 – 1**). During that ride, he actually turned the controls over to me. Fantastic! At the Colonel's home, he and his wife entertained Colonel Anderson, his wife, myself and Delores. Delores or Dee was a young lady that I had met in Denver and I invited her to join me for dinner. Of course, the conversation at the table centered around my resignation and what I was going to do, post Academy. I could see out of the corner of my eye that Dee was liking the way the conversation was going. Both Colonels were putting up very strong arguments, possibly stronger than what she could have or had done. I noticed that a smile began to creep across her face.   The highlight of the argument didn't come from Dee, or the two Colonels, but from the wife of the colonel who was hosting us. She had quietly removed herself from the table, was gone for about five minutes and returned. When she came back, she laid two keys down on the table. She immediately got all of our attention. She looked at me and said in a very quiet voice,

"Mel, here are two keys. One key is to an extra car that we have. While you are here, and you may use that car anytime you wish. The other key is to our Mother-in-law suite. We don't have a Mother-in-Law, so it is sitting empty. That key will provide you access anytime you want. Just keep it clean." She went and sat back down. How do you top that? Everybody was smiling except for me.

General Olds

It is important to know the background, history, and temperament of the person that I had to speak to for my "Exit Interview." His name is General Robin Olds.

Robin Olds (July 14, 1922 – June 14, 2007) was an American fighter pilot and general officer in the U.S. Air force. He was a "Triple Ace" with a combined total of 16 victories in WW II and the Vietnam war. He retired in 1973 as a Brigadier General.

The son of regular Army Maj. Gen. Robert Olds, educated at West Point, and the product of an upbringing in the early years of the U.S. Army Corps. Olds epitomized the youthful World War II fighter pilot. He remained in the service as it became the U.S. Air Force despite often being at odds with its leadership, and was one of its pioneer jet pilots. Rising to command of two fighter wings, Olds is regarded among aviation historians and his peers as the best wing commander of the Vietnam War, both for his air-fighting skills and his reputation as a combat leader.

Olds was promoted to Brigadier General after returning from Vietnam but did not hold another major command. The remainder of his career was spent in non-operational positions, as Commandant of Cadets at the U.S. Air Force Academy and as an official in the Air Force Inspector's General Office. His inability to rise higher as a general officer is attributed to both his maverick views and his penchant for drinking.

Olds had a highly publicized career and life, including marriage to Hollywood actress Ella Raines. As a young man he was also recognized for his athletic prowess in both high school and college, being named an All American for his play as a lineman in American football. Olds expressed his philosophy regarding fighter pilots in the quote: "There are pilots and there are pilots; with the good ones, it is inborn. You can't teach it. If you are a fighter pilot, you have to be willing to take risks."

The Final Chapter – Exit Interview

The day came that I go to meet the colonel that performs the exit interviews. Colonel Anderson had requested that I stop by to see him before I went in.

We talked a little bit, and then he said, "stop by again afterwards."

I left the colonel's office and went to see the exit officer. Standing outside of his office, I was informed that I would not see the colonel, but that I would meet with Brig. General Olds instead. General Olds was a fighter pilot in Vietnam and is the Commandant of Cadets. Essentially, all cadets ultimately reported to Gen. Olds. A doolie meeting with Gen. Olds is un-heard of. I go over to the wing of the Admin building that houses Gen. Olds' office and encounter his adjutant, a colonel. The colonel was sitting outside the General's office and was a little gruff. After all, I am but a Doolie, frequently ignored and seldom recognized. My appearance at the General's office could only mean trouble. The Colonel told me to go into the office. I stood in the door way and knocked. I immediately took in the picture before me. A good-sized man, with his legs and boots (yes, cowboy boots in particular) resting on top of his desk, on the phone, leaning back in his chair that was adorned with four red stars. The stars signified the four planes that he shot down while flying over Vietnam in the F-4 Phantom. He continued to talk on the phone as he waved me in.

I took two steps, went to attention, saluted and proceeded to say, "Sir, Cadet King is reporting as ordered, Sir."

I got as far as "Sir, Cadet King...) when he waved me off and pointed to a chair. His phone call un-interrupted.

When he completed his phone conversation, he said, "So, you're the Cadet King. I have been reviewing your folder."

The General said, "I have your personnel folder, and I have been reviewing it. Actually, its quite unusual, especially for a Doolie."

I didn't know how to take his remark since it was neutral and could go either way. I sat quietly and didn't say anything. His pause was not very long.

He continued to say, "Are you aware what your squad did for the Challenge Course? Completing seven out of the 15? First time that it had ever been done. Are you aware that no one in your squad had gotten a gig slip? No, you wouldn't know that. Are you aware that your squad is considered one of the top squads at the Academy? No, you wouldn't know that either. We started checking into why the squad you are in was doing so well. It didn't take long before it was determined that you were the differential factor. We found out you gave classes on shoe shinning, bed making, dusting, cleaning, etc., etc. You took these 17 – 18-year-olds under your wing and without reservation or hesitation, transferred whatever knowledge or experience you had to them. One cadet told us a story when you and he were running 'point' for your squad. It was an exercise where you were a part of Company A, going against Company B. The two of you were a good 50 -70 yards out front of your squad when you heard troops coming in the opposite direction. Unfortunately, you were caught out in a clearing with nowhere to go. In just three to five seconds the opposing troops would round a bend and would spot the two of you immediately. You would have been either captured or marked as a casualty. He told us that you gave him quick instructions of which he complied. To his amazement, the troops past you by, and now that the two of you were behind the opposing troops, you were able to challenge the troops to surrender. They did. We are certain that none of the other cadets would have known what to do in that situation. Frankly, we are amazed that you did. We have been watching you, you and your squad."

General Olds

General Olds said, "Are you aware that you have been selected to be appointed a temporary Cadet Captain while the Upperclassmen are gone for Thanksgiving holiday? Given command of your flight? What is also amazing is that you have been rated 83rd in your class, out of 1200 cadets. This also is unheard of. When a Doolie submits his resignation, he is doing well to stay out of the bottom 10%, let alone be rated among the top 10%. When I first picked up your file, I was curious why it was sent over and why it had a red dot on it. You see, it is very unusual for a resignation to be sent to the office of the Commandant of Cadets. As I read your file, I began to understand why it was sent to me; and, why it had a red dot. The red dot is a code. It means, 'keep at all cost.' Your file was sent to me so that I could exert influence in having you stay at the Academy. So, I'm in the act of twisting your arm to encourage you to stay."

The General went on to describe the difference in my life as an Air Force officer and that being a civilian. He was right in many things. *The service does and has recognized your innate leadership; which, may not necessarily be so in the civilian sector where politics and envy can come into play; and is more decisive."* Still, the more he talked about my 'not making it' the more my resolve was to prove him, and many others wrong.

After about 20 minutes of his outlining my future life, he said, "I have been speaking long enough; you tell me why you want to leave the Academy."

I had been in the General's office for about 40 minutes now and up to this time, I may have spoken a total of 25 words. I began to say why I was resigning and got out about another 25 words when the General stood up.

"Well, it doesn't matter the reason, I'm not accepting your resignation." He said.

I stood up out of my seat, leaned over his desk and said, "You what, you can't do that."

"But I just did. I'm going to give you more time to think about it, and give you until the end of the semester, at Christmas. By the time you write your congressman and get a reply, it'll be Christmas anyway, so you may as well accept the fact that you're not going anywhere before Christmas. You come back then; and, if you still want to go, I'll sign your resignation."

He got out of his chair, put his arm around me, said some words that I didn't hear, didn't want to hear, and walked me to the door. He got me just beyond the threshold, and closed his door. I'm standing there, fuming, with my nose about two inches from the door. The Colonel who was sitting right outside the door, looked at me, started to say something, I looked at him with a "don't you dare" look. He looked back at his desk, began doing some work, all with a big grin across his face. He totally ignored me while I stood, face at the door. I don't know how long I stood there, but eventually, the Colonel (General Olds adjutant) got out of his chair, put his arm around me and escorted me out of the office.

"Have a good day cadet." He said.

I slowly walked back to Colonel Anderson's office feeling totally dejected. Colonel Anderson was on the phone, so I stood at attention just outside his office. While still on the phone he motioned for me to come in and have a seat. I went in and sat down.

"Well, how did it go?" the Colonel asked.

"He didn't accept my resignation." I replied, gritting my teeth.

The Colonel didn't quite hear, so he asked me to repeat myself.

In a much louder voice, but still with clenched teeth, "I said, he didn't accept my resignation."

As I mentioned earlier, Col. Anderson was responsible for administration. There were about 30 people working in the office area. Colonel Anderson is a big man; about six feet six, 260 pounds with an athletic build. Me, I was six feet and about 170 pounds. When the Colonel laughs, he has this big, loud, baritone laughter. When Colonel Anderson started laughing, the whole office stopped. Now imagine the scene that the office people saw. This huge colonel grabbing his sides from laughing so hard, and in comparison, this pipsqueak Doolie, sitting in a chair, slumped over, grimacing. What could be more incongruous? Colonel got up out of his seat, still laughing and went over to close his door. The office staff was still starring. I'm sure they all thought, "Never seen this happen before."

Colonel said, "Now tell me what happened; and, don't leave anything out."

I started by saying, "First I went to the Colonel's office responsible for discharging cadets. But I never saw him, they took me immediately to see General Olds, and..."

"You What!? They took you to see General Olds? Whoa boy, that's a new one. Now this is really getting interesting. I didn't even know they had you scheduled to see the General. OK, well tell me, what happened next?"

I told Colonel all the things that they were tracking about me, the comments from my peers and where I was rated amongst my class. I think even the Colonel was impressed as he sat there with a huge grin on his face.

When I finished, he said, "This calls for a celebration dinner at my house. You and a guest are invited. I'll let you know the date."

There was not much more for me to do than to accept the invitation. As I got up to leave, Colonel said, "Mel, I want you to know, I only know of one other time in the Academy's history that a resignation was refused; and, that was for a heavily recruited football player. You achieved something amazing today. Think on it."

That Christmas, I saw General Olds again. He signed the papers.

My decision to leave the academy was based on the subtle changes in personality that I didn't realize was happening but family and others were beginning to notice; and, it wasn't nice. Also, I was being asked to discriminate against enlisted personnel, friends that I had at the Prep School, of whom that I no longer could associate. I have been the target of discrimination and I for sure did not want to be the initiator of such behavior.

McGuire AFB – First Sergeant

The following January, 1970, I reported in at McGuire AFB, in New Jersey. And, as usual, I had my initial Faux Pas at the beginning of my assignment.   It happened at my first Commander's call. I was on base for about two weeks when the First Sergeant and the Squadron Commander held a meeting in the base auditorium for all airmen within the Commander's command. On this occasion, the Colonel had not arrived yet, so I think the First Sergeant took opportunity of the Commander's absence.

The First Sergeant was in front of the auditorium, pacing back and forth, telling about 450 of us saying,

"Do you Airmen know how tough my job is? The hours I have to put in, the weekends I have to give up, the decisions I have to make, etc."

It was a real sob story. I guess he was starting to wind down when he asked the question, "Which one of you think you could do my job."

I didn't know it was a rhetorical question, meaning he wasn't really looking for an answer. Anyhow, my hand went up…until I noticed that my hand was the *only* hand that went up. I started lowering my hand so the First Sergeant wouldn't see it. Too late. The Sarge was over on the left side of the auditorium, I was sitting on the right side about three rows back. The Sarge ran over to where I was sitting, read my name tag.

"King huh. Well Sergeant King, you got yourself a job this weekend. I needed to be home on Friday, so this is going to work out great. You'll report to my office bright and early on Friday, assume my responsibilities and be on call for the weekend. I'll get a de-brief from you on Monday."

The room was quiet. About then the Commander walked in. Of course, after the meeting, you can imagine the ribbing I got.

That Friday I went to the First Sergeants office to assume my/ his duties. I got a cold reception from the office staff, but went into the Sarge's office and sat behind his desk. I looked at his calendar for the day's meeting and began to review some of the paperwork. First appointment was a Master Sergeant who was retiring. The Master Sergeant knocked on the door. My desk was situated as such that a person could not see in to see if someone was at the desk or not.

I said, "Come in."

As he entered, the look on the Master Sergeants face was priceless.

He looked at me, stepped back, looked at the title and name on the door, and said, "Am I in the right place?" I stood up, walked around the desk and extended my hand.

"Yes, you are. Sarge took the weekend off."

After 30 years of service, here he is being checked out by a kid less than half his age. We talked a little while and he got around to asking how I ended up behind the desk. I told him. He began laughing and almost couldn't stop. Because of his laughter, one of my/ Sarge's assistants came and closed the door. As we finished, I walked him to the outer office and we shook hands. The fact that this Master Sergeant left with a smile on his face and a little laughter thawed the office a little. I had some more papers to sign until my next appointment, a young airman on his first assignment. He shows up at the door, knocks and begins to enter upon my acknowledgement. He takes his first step, sees me, backs up, looks to see if he is in the right office, turns and asks one of the assistants if the First Sergeant was in. With a brief chuckle, the assistant informs the airman that I am acting First Sergeant and instructed him to go into the office. He, still with a puzzled look on his face, entered the office. Since he didn't ask, I didn't address his unasked question, "How did you come about being a First Sergeant?" The airman's plight was his haircut. The "Afro" look, although popular in the civilian world, was just becoming popular in the military; and more and more Black Airmen were wearing an Afro. His was relatively short, neatly trimmed and very stylish. Problem was, his sergeant didn't like it. I got up from behind my desk, checked him out really good.

"Hmmm… I like it. I like it a lot. In fact, where did you get it cut?" I said.

He looked at me with astonishment. I wrote down the location. Then I wrote a memo to his sergeant that went something like this, "Airman Johnson's haircut is neatly trimmed, at reasonable length and is acceptable within the unit of this command."
The airman read the note and grew a Cheshire cat's smile and left the office with a bounce to his step. Ahhh, being First Sergeant had its advantages. I just set the standard on the base for Afro haircuts for all Black airmen, self-included.

Later that day, I had to accompany the Commander for a "Commander's Tour" of the barracks. The Commander, as with most of the people in the office, was very stiff and very formal with me. However, as we began to talk, and he found out I had a tour in Southeast Asia and had just left the Air Force Academy, he thawed immeasurably. I even told him about General Olds and his cowboy boots. As we made the tour, the Colonel became very comfortable in our conversation; and cut our tour short, just so that we could have an extended time at lunch to talk. He had a lot of questions, so I did most of the talking. Near the end of the conversation, he attempted to get me to re-enlist. However, I asked him about the logic of re-enlisting as an enlisted person, having passed up the opportunity to become an officer.

He thought about that, "Well, I'll submit your name for officer school."

He said in earnest. Soon after, the Commander and I went back to the office. When the people in the office saw how the Colonel and I were relating, they immediately changed their disposition toward me. They had thawed a little earlier, but this was a complete melt-down. Office politics. Once the melt-down occurred, I made my rounds with the office staff. I think many of them enjoyed the brief respite. The rest of the afternoon went by very quickly, and many of the office personnel came by to say "Good night" and how they enjoyed having me in the office. My job wasn't over yet. I was on stand-by for the weekend. Meaning, I couldn't leave the base and always had to be near a phone (cell phones didn't exist). Fortunately, it was a quiet weekend. On Monday, I met the real First Sergeant and gave him a report of what happened while he was away. He told me he called in a couple of times on Friday and was surprised by the positive comments he got. He told me that if ever I needed assistance or help with anything, that I was to see him first.

He said, "We don't get very many in the service like you, certainly would like to keep you. But I already spoke to the Colonel and he told me about his conversation with you. Anyhow, I mean it. If you ever need anything, come see me."

I left the office and reported back to my shop on the flightline.

Corrosion Control/ Paint Shop

The nature of my AFSC (Air Force Specialty Code) had grown since the two of us had reported in at Seymour-Johnson AFB, a few years back. There we about 12 of us in the shop with a Tech Sergeant in charge. However, I was still the ranking airman with technical training in our AFSC. We had the responsibility to ensure the flight integrity of the huge C-141 cargo planes and a variety of other aircraft. The C-141 was a beautiful aircraft (see **Fig 39-1**).   I was always amazed at the size and payload of cargo it could carry. We would crawl all over this aircraft, looking for tiny cracks or corrosion. Depending on the location, if we saw a crack developing, we would do what any woman wearing stockings would do when she saw a "run", we would put a hole at the end of the run to terminate it. It may seem strange, but we would get a drill and drill a small whole at the end of the crack to prevent it from continuing. It works. We also did Dye Penetrant Inspection and other stuff to make sure the C-141s stayed in the air. One thing about the plane I thought was cool, the ladder in the tail, with a hatch on top. I always volunteered or gave myself the assignment to inspect the tail so I could climb to the top, open the hatch, and look around from this vantage point.

Fig. 39-1, C-141 Star lifter

I was in the shop for about three months when the chief or Tech Sergeant called me to the shop office.

He said, "Mel, we've been watching you work and want to give you an opportunity to head up a unit. We want to put you in charge of stripping, prepping and repainting the C-141's. It will be your shop, yours to work however you want."

I don't remember exactly how many people worked that part of the shop, maybe 10 – 12, but I do remember it had four civilians working. That could be a challenge. The whole cycle of stripping, prepping, and repainting a C-141 took six weeks. I obviously didn't have a choice in the matter so I graciously accepted the "opportunity" and told him I would do my best. The Sarge took me over to introduce me to my new crew. Many of the guys I knew, but only as their peer. This would be different. After the Sarge left, I got the team together, including the civilians.

I said, "We are going to have a brain storming session."

"A what?" Was the immediate response.

"We are going to get in a room and talk about how we can do this job better, faster, easier…and I want your input."

"Yea, right." They'd heard that comment before.

We found an empty classroom with chalk and a blackboard (Yes, blackboard). I told the team I thought we could do better than six weeks. But before we started the session, I asked a few questions.

One question I asked was "How many lived within a 100-mile radius?"

Most of the hands went up.

I then asked, "How many have had the opportunity to go home for the weekend?"

Surprisingly few raised their hands. Most of the airmen in the room were junior airmen and oftentimes were picked to work the weekend shift.

"How would you like to go home or at least get away for the weekend?"

All hands went up.

"If I can get it so that you can get off every-other weekend, would that be incentive enough for you to work faster and better than you have been before?"

A resounding "Yes."

"Now, let's see if we can throw out some ideas to make it happen. Let's set our goal for a four-week cycle instead of six. As for the civilians, we need your help if these guys are going to get some benefit. Since your skill set is critical to keep things flowing, we need you to change your timing a little. Rather than you taking smoke breaks at any time during the day, we need to have set times. You guys pick two times in the morning and two times after lunch that you all go together. That way we don't get interrupted with one of you being gone, at odd times, while the rest of us wait."

The civilians agreed to set a schedule; then we started throwing out ideas. We finished the session with plans to implement the ideas on the next aircraft. Everybody was pumped.

Two weeks later, we got our chance. We implemented the new ideas and completed the whole cycle in four weeks and two days. Not bad for the first time out. The Sarge was watching the airmen and civilians working together and was surprised to see our progress. As promised, I was able to give all the airmen the weekend off, and the civilians got off half day on Friday. The whole team was ecstatic. Before everyone left for the weekend, we did a "lessons learned" to see how we could improve on our performance for the next plane. The second plane that came through we did in three and half weeks. It quickly became a challenge to us to improve our performance after each plane.

When we got to three weeks, the Colonel came out to thank us for cutting the time in half. We didn't stop there. We got it to two weeks and two days. The Colonel came out again and jokingly said that if we got any faster, we would run out of C-141's. We did. We got faster and we ran out of C-141's. We were able to complete the full cycle time in one and ½ weeks. We worked a few more hours during the week, but the airmen felt that it was a good tradeoff. Occasionally, and depending on the availability of the aircraft, I would give them Friday off as well for a three-day weekend. At some point during this responsibility, the leadership team replaced me with a Tech Sergeant (two grades above me) and re-assigned me to lead just one of the elements. Not sure how it happened, but in two weeks when we would normally be finished with an aircraft, we were only half way through the project. The Colonel and First Sergeant met with me and asked if I could determine what the problem was and resume the leadership of the project.

"Also, Sergeant King, since you will be leaving us soon, identify who your replacement is going to be and begin training him."

I accepted the leadership once again and picked my replacement. I stayed at this assignment until my departure from the service.

Off Hours

While at McGuire AFB, I met a sergeant, whom I'll call Ben, of whom we became very good friends. He had a new, yellow, Plymouth Roadrunner that we would often go into Camden or Trenton, New Jersey. One Saturday, we stopped by to visit a couple of girls that we recently met at a dance. They lived in a very nice neighborhood and their house was well kept. We walked up the sidewalk, to the porch, and rang the doorbell. Their dog, tongue hanging out, jumped to its feet when the doorbell rang. One the girls greeted us, opened the door for us and their dog, and we went in. We spent about an hour getting better acquainted and made plans to get together soon. While we were talking, we notice their dog was a little rambunctious, not much, but could have been more under control. Just as we got up to leave, and being polite, we asked them what was the name of their dog.

"Our dog? Isn't it your dog?"

As the realization of what just happened came to all of us, we began laughing so hard our sides started hurting. We began mimicking the antics of the dog and commenting on what it must have been thinking.

"Wow, these are really nice people. Boy, this sofa sure is soft. I wonder when are they going to break out the chow? Etc."

On the way back to McGuire, and although Ben and I enjoyed the ladies' company, I think we talked more about the dog.

A month before I left McGuire, Ben and I had another date in Camden. It was scheduled for 8:00 PM on a Saturday. The time was 8:15 PM and no Ben. This was not like Ben. At 8:30 PM I called our dates, apologized, told them that I had not heard from Ben and I don't know what happened. Around 10:30 PM I decided that I may as well get some sleep. About 11:30 PM I get a phone call. It was the base hospital. They told me that they had Sergeant Ben, that he was in a car accident, and was in critical condition. They said the only name they could get out of him was mine. I was asked to come to the hospital immediately as that may increase his survival instincts. I borrowed a car from another friend, and raced to the hospital. Ben was in bad condition. I found out later what happened. Earlier that day, two other guys wanted to go into Trenton. While in town, they stopped at this bar and began to have a couple of drinks. Problem was, they all began to drink. Whenever Ben and I went out, he would always give me the car keys. I never drank more than one of anything, and was the defacto designated driver. On this occasion, Ben, recognizing his own limitation, and as he usually did with me, gave the car keys to one of the other two airmen.

You may not be familiar with a Plymouth Roadrunner. The Roadrunner was a muscle car and could compete with the Mustang, Camaro, and Charger. So, the stage is set for a major catastrophe. A high-powered vehicle, in the hands of a young driver, and a driver who drunk too much. While at the hospital, a cop was there and he told me what happened. On the way back to the base from Trenton, they were traveling on a winding back road in excess of 80 miles per hour when it left the road, went airborne, went down an embankment, cut several saplings in half, plowed through bushes, continuing to roll into a ball, and came to a rest over 300 ft from the road. When the police arrived, they were in recovery mode (as in bodies), not rescue. They couldn't believe anyone could have survived this crash. Miracles upon miracles. Consensus from the doctors is that all three survived because they all were intoxicated and did not tense up but remained flexible. Ben was lying down in the back seat, so he never saw, nor knew what happened. That morning I called the First Sergeant (how ironic, he was on weekend call) and told him what happened. I then asked if he would write a memo to excuse me for a couple of days while I played nursemaid to try to get my friend to pull through.

The Sergeant said, "Sergeant King, I told you, all you have to do is ask. Consider it done. And besides, we don't want to lose one of our own. You stay with him until you determine it is OK to leave."

Ben slipped in and out of a coma for the next couple of days. On the third day, he came fully awake, wondering why he was in the hospital. I told him what the police told us, which was the back end. I asked him about the front end. Collectively, we were able to put all the pieces together for a complete story.

I told him, "The one time you go into Trenton without me and look what happened. You just can't be trusted."

Departure

My termination from the service was fairly anti-climactic. About two weeks before I got out, I bought a used Opel Kadet. I later found out that it wouldn't re-start after the engine got hot and I couldn't go over 55 MPH without the whole body shaking. Before I left the base for the final time, with my newly purchased used car, I stopped by the hospital. Ben was given a good prognosis from the doctors. They said he was just going to be spending a few months in rehab, but should fully recover. We said our good byes, and I wished him well. I got in my car and began heading west. I set my sights on my first stop, Indianapolis where I would stay a day with my brother, on to Denver where I would spend a couple of days with some friends there, and then on to LA. The whole trip, I couldn't go faster than 55 MPH. I had no thought about cops.

The following story is an excerpt of one of my childhood adventures

38[Th] St. Go-Kart & the Night

It was a rare rainy summer day in Los Angeles. One of those days that seemed liked imprisonment. We gathered at the window, Dickie, Leroy, Juan, Larry, and I, and with elongated faces looked at the grey, depressing overcast sky. It wasn't fair, it hadn't rained for a couple of months and today of all days. For today, we were going to try out our new and improved go-kart. This was no ordinary go-kart, this one had breaks. You know, like in breaks that make you stop. Sure, we added some trim and a new horn but the breaks were just way too cool. Understand, we didn't have Big-Wheels, motorized cars that looked like the family vehicle or manufactured scooters. If we wanted something to ride in or on, other than a bike, we had to build it, and build it we did.

One of the most important parts of the go-kart is the shoe-skate. Shoe-skates, what is a shoe-skate? Other than providing the wheels to the go-kart, shoe-skates are special because their offering requires a sacrifice and a passion of commitment to build the go-kart. Sacrifice, because once donated, they rarely returned in the form that  they were given. Passion, because the skates helped to promote the common good and exploration for those of us who lived or played on or around 38th street. The shoe-skates were all metal monsters that, with a skate-key, were able to clamp to tennis shoes, school shoes, church shoes or anything else that went on your feet. We even tried it without shoes. Doesn't work. Anyhow, each skate separates into two parts. The back half was used for the rear of the go-kart while the front was used for the steer-able cross member of the go-kart. Go-karts were simple to construct, especially when your dad owned a cabinet and wood working shop.

Construction of the go-kart always started out at my dad's shop. My dad always kept a bin full of scrap wood that we were free to use (never thought about it much then, but somehow, we were always able to find a two-, four- and six-foot length of 2X4 in the scrap bin). We might have to remove a few nails, but we always found the wood, and at the right length. We'd nail the short two-foot piece at one end of the six-foot length, making a cross with about a two inch over hang. This two-inch overhang was done to protect the bike reflector (also sacrificed) that would be attached to the short cross member. Then we'd get dad's drill and drill a ¼ or 5/8th inch hole about six inches from the other end of the six-foot 2X4. This hole would be needed to allow steering of the kart. Afterwards, we would drill a hole right in the middle of the four-foot 2X4. Finally, we would scrounge around to find four washers, a long enough bolt and a nut. The bolt with a washer went through the long 2X4, followed by two washers (these permitted less friction), the four-foot 2X4, the last washer

Our go-kart was similar to this except we had to use shoe-skates instead of wheels.

and then the nut. This assembly was the basic steering unit of the go-kart. (After a few models and abruptly losing our front axles, we learned to use lock washers on the bottom of the bolt.) Once we got this far, it was a solemn moment, for now it required the sacrifice of the shoe-skate.

Up to this point, the shoe-skate belonged to an individual, but now it was a sacrifice for the common good. More often than not, the skates usually were Leroy's. Leroy lived alone with his dad and he, unlike most of us, always seemed to have money. We never begged him for any money nor held it against him, we just thought that some things he could sacrifice easier than the rest of us... shoe-skates being one of them. I often wondered what his dad thought he was doing with the skates, I mean, after all they were metal and not easy to tear up.

After the skates, we would find two triangle pieces of wood about six inches on both sides and nail them to the frame and the seat back. The seat back was also used as a stop to push the go-kart. Our motor was whoever was the junior kid or rookie in the neighborhood. We'd find an old broom, cut off the head and use the handle as a push rod. This way we would not have to bend over and could run faster while pushing. This was the basic design, everything else was customizing. We talked about putting in for a patent for this design until we heard that patents cost a thousand dollars. Oh well.

With the push pole, the basic design was complete. Often times we would customize our carts by putting a hood over the front, tin cans for headlights, bicycle horn, streamers and a lot of other cool stuff. We were like nature and snowflakes; no two go-karts were ever alike.

Once the karts were built, we would take it out on our test track. Larry lived next to this big parking lot that belonged to the place where his dad worked. (As we got older, we use to help park cars there. In fact, I learned to drive a stick on that lot... but that's another story).   It was perfect for our testing grounds. It was long enough for us to get up to speed and wide enough to give us a safety margin as we tested the steering assembly. Sometimes, when we first use the go-kart, the steering would freeze. When this happens, we would pull with all our might on one side of the rope. Sometimes it began to turn very slowly, other times it wouldn't budge. Bail out time. Just for this reason, our first run would always be toward the closed end of the track. The other end was opened and the beasts of the streets would patrol at frequent intervals.

We always had safety in mind, so we stayed away from that end. Back to the trouble at hand. Dickey was in the kart, and the steering assembly was not working. No steering, bailout time. Bailing out of a moving go-kart was not an easy thing to do. Timing had to be just right. Just before the end of the test track there was about six feet of grass and dirt mixture. This was the bailout area. After this was a four-foot-high fence. Bail out too soon and you land on blacktop, too late and you'll end up in the fence along with the go-kart. Now mind you, we just couldn't bailout, we had to bail out with style. We kept points from all our adventures so when we bailed, we didn't want to look like a rag doll. Thus far, Dickey had the most points and after this crash, he added a bunch to his total. We ran up to Dickey and asked him why he didn't use the new brakes. This was the first model to have brakes and Dickey just plain forgot about them. He got a good score for style points, minus points for not using the breaks.

After the repair and the go-kart passed the readiness test, it was ready for the race track. Dickey, being the oldest, had first ride. Juan, being the youngest had first push. I was on the bike and had scouting duty. Leroy had on some real skates (the kind that lace up) and brought up the rear. Randy who had neither bike nor skates would occasionally help Juan with pushing the kart. We had quite a way to go. We had to go several blocks to Vermont Ave., cross a huge section of the L.A. Coliseum parking lot to Menlo Blvd, pass between two museums and the Coliseum, finally, around to the front of the Coliseum, through several

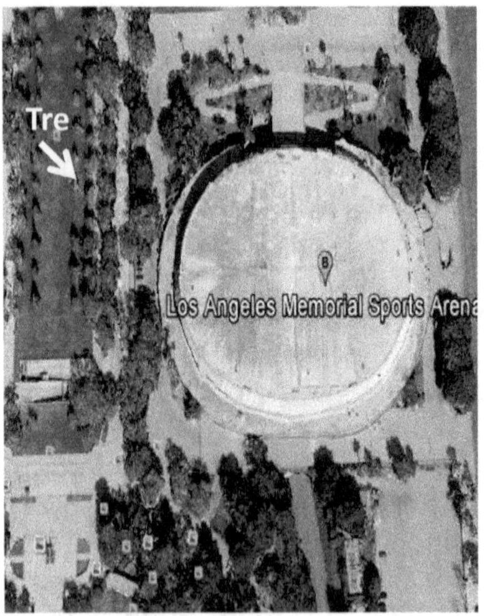

rows of ancient and humongous pine trees, and from there to the front of the sports arena.

The L.A. Lakers, USC basketball and the Kings play here in the Sports Arena (until the Inglewood Forum was built). It is a multipurpose facility and gets a lot of usage.

Because we had that steering problem, we didn't get to the race track as early as we wanted. It was late afternoon, but since it was summer, we still had plenty of daylight left. Now you may have asked "why the Sports Arena?" Well, in the front of the arena, there are two, very wide opposing ramps that are shaped like a giant "U" or "V." People use these ramps to access the lower level of the arena, or to leave the lower levels to go up to ground level. In total there is about a 20 - 25-foot drop with this U-turn right in the middle. It took a lot of skill to navigate the U-turn and to maintain speed. We would time each other to see who could do it faster. We used the tried and true, one-thousand one, one-thousand two, one-thousand three…. Anyhow, this day we were expecting to set a new world's record. And sure nuff, the brakes were letting us take the U-turn faster and faster.

Finally, after numerous new records, Dickey wanted one last try to smash our previous marks. Besides, it was starting to turn to dusk and surely, we didn't want to walk past the museums in the dark. We always talked about what happens in museums when everyone leaves. Bru-uther, it gives me the hebegeebies just thinking about it. Well, Dickey said he want to smash the earlier marks. So, in order to do this, we were going to give him a running start. Normally we would position the kart just at the top of the ramp and give a small push. From there, gravity would do its thing. This time however, we were going to use Newton's law of apples, that is, "things that fall want to keep falling." So, rather than place the kart at the top of the ramp, we backed the kart up about 20 feet. The Olympic bobsledding teams had nothing on us. We were ready, Dickey was ready, the kart was ready.

"On my mark, …set…go!" Dickey said.

The acceleration was phenomenal. Dickey was hunkered down behind the hood, hands tight on the steering rope, and a look of determination couldn't have fit anyone else's face

better. Boy, we knew a new record would be set. Unfortunately, none of us were engineers. We knew nothing about failure testing, stress testing or even using dummies for testing. I guess, in a way, we were the dummies. Well, Dickey continued to gather speed at a tremendous rate; and, we saw a phenomenon that we had never seen before. Dickey was going so fast that he was raising dust up off the ground. We instantly declared that this run would set a new "Dust Record."   Dust was flying, Dickey was still hunkered down, the kart was gaining more speed and looking good.

The moment of truth. The U-turn. With a confidence and skill that we all attributed to Dickey being older than the rest of us, he initiated the turn sequence. The turn sequence: grabbing the rope with one hand at unequal distances, free the other hand and position it on the brakes, prepare to pull the rope and applying the brakes at the same time to send the kart into a slide.   Done correctly this slide will permit the kart to make the turn with minimal loss of speed. Remember, we were not engineers.

As Dickey applied the brakes and pulled on the rope, two things happened that resulted in a third thing. The first of the two things was that the speed caused the brakes to fail. The second thing was that the steering mechanism chose that moment to freeze.   The resultant third thing was that the kart obeyed Newton's fallen apple theory – it kept going, straight that is, yielding to the laws of gravity. This was the second time we saw dust that day. We immediately began running down the ramp. While the dust was settling, we didn't know if Dickey survived or not. What we finally saw was Dickey draped "U" shaped over the handrails, arms extended downward as if in the "I surrender" position.   His eyes were closed and we wondered if he was breathing. A brief argument broke out as to whom would apply mouth-to-mouth CPR if needed. Fortunately, for us or him, I don't know which, his eyes opened. We helped him from the railing and surveyed the damage to the kart. Except for the brakes, the kart was repairable. When you keep things simple, it makes repairing equally simple. It took a while but we fixed the kart to the degree that we could ride it home, and once there do a major overhaul.

By now, it was past the time to leave. The sun was setting. So, our rag tag crew, me on the bike, Leroy on skates, Dickey in the kart with Juan and Randy pushing, set off for home. The crash and the repair of the kart really delayed us. Although none of us said it, we all thought it, now we were going to have to go by the museum while it was dark. We always fantasized about all the animals and weird stuff in the museum coming alive. So, passing by the museum at night would be a challenge for us. (The movie, "Night at the Museum" didn't have anything on us... They just made money. Oh well.) Well, we started our journey home. It's amazing how something so majestic and awesome during the day can be so sinister, scary, and intimidating at night. Those big 'ol pine trees in the front of the Coliseum looked like they had hands for branches; and, as the wind blew them, it looked like the hands were reaching for us. We didn't go through the trees like we did when we came, we went around them.

We proceeded to walk, bike, skate, and ride next to the fence that surrounded the Coliseum. While everyone was focused on the museums, I was looking in the Coliseum. I learned from plenty of John Wayne war movies that everybody shouldn't be looking in the same direction. Never can tell what might sneak up on you. As I looked in the Coliseum, I saw something flash by one of the tunnels.

I cried out, "Guys, did you see that?" (We were at position "**1**", what I saw was at "**A**")

"Nah, didn't see a thing. You're just trying to scare us." Someone replied.

No one else saw what I saw. We all became wary and very watchful. We must have traveled about 50 yards (**2**) when I looked behind us.

"Guys look at that!" I said.

What we saw was a figure in black (**B**) that seemed to be floating about a foot above the ground. We saw no legs or nothing touching the ground. Bicycle, skates, go-kart and all began to move at a high rate of speed.   The third time dust was seen that day.

Leroy's skates were flying, my legs on the bike were a blur, Juan and Randy, pushing Dickey in the go-kart, were with us neck and neck. Now it seems strange that four different modes of travel, bike, skates, running and pushing a go-kart would all be equal in speed. How could we all be together? What happened next could only happen if all of us were traveling at the same rate of speed. Leroy's legs were going wild, so wild that he hit the front wheel of my bike, that caused me to wobble and cross the path of the kart, the kart ran over my front wheel, causing the kart to stop, which in turn caused the pushers, Randy and Juan to fall forward. The result, after about a 100-yard dash, we all ended up in one big heap (**3**). Bike, skate, go-kart, and runners jumbled up together. We were in this pile sorting ourselves out for just a few seconds when, what we were running from was upon us (**C**). A little old lady, dressed in black, said as she peered at each of us.

"Little boys like you shouldn't be out at night." She said.

Open mouth and slack jawed we said nothing. We couldn't say anything. We immediately got up, put the kart in some nearby bushes and ran to the corner to see where this little old lady got to. From the corner of Menlo Street and 39th, you can see this huge parking lot on both sides of the street and the fencing that goes around the Coliseum. A person would have to travel at least 200 yards in plain sight before they reached a building, trees or some other obstruction. Well, we ran to the corner and looked. We looked in every direction and saw no old lady. In fact, we saw no one, neither in the parking lots nor by the fencing surrounding the Coliseum. We all agreed that an old woman couldn't move that fast. Yet we all knew that she caught up to us, when we had all fallen, in a matter of seconds. Okay, okay, we knew then that we either saw a ghost or an angel. We all agreed, however, whatever it was, it wasn't human.

As we went go-karting, for the rest of the summer, we made sure we were home an hour before sundown.

www.ingramcontent.com/pod-product-compliance
Lightning Source LLC
Chambersburg PA
CBHW060939050726
47592CB00003B/1030